DETOX *Style*

Creating A Healthy Lifestyle Through Daily Holistic Detoxification Practices

DR. T. HOUSTON, ND, MDiv.

Detox-Style: Creating a Healthy Lifestyle through Daily Holistic Detoxification Practices

Journey of Wellness Natural Medicine Center, LLC
P.O. Box 82346
Conyers, GA 30013

DISCLAIMER

The information written in this book is based on the education, research, and experience of the author and is therefore not intended to replace visits to a licensed healthcare professional. The information in this book is not intended to diagnose, treat, or cure any medical condition. This information is to be used as a resource of health information only in conjunction with your visits to qualified healthcare professionals.

ISBN-13: 978-1539595090

ISBN-10: 1539595099

DETOX-STYLE

(n.) The habits of regular holistic detoxification as a way of life; a detoxification lifestyle.

(v.)Participating in holistic habits and practices of detoxification as a way of life.

PILLARS OF DETOX-STYLE

1. **IDENTIFY** your daily controllable toxic exposures

2. **LIMIT** your daily exposures to toxins as much as possible

3. **SUPPORT** your detoxification pathways daily through diet, movement, water, and self-expression

4. **CLEANSE** your whole health with supportive therapies at regular intervals

CONTENTS

PREFACE   V

ABOUT THE AUTHOR'S HOLISTIC JOURNEY   VII

DEDICATION   XIII

INTRODUCTION   XIX

PART 1: CUMULATIVE TOXIC EXPOSURES
AND ITS IMPACT ON HEALTH   1

CHAPTER 1: CONTROLLING DISEASE VS. PROMOTING HEALTH   3
The World Health Organization ~ Cumulative Effect of Toxins ~ Toxic Presentations in the Body ~ Toxic Impact on Organ Systems

CHAPTER 2: TOXIC BUILDUP & ITS THREAT TO THE FAMILY   11
Endocrine Disruptors ~ Embryo Fetus ~ Infants and Children ~ Women's Health ~ Men's Health

PART 2: DAILY TOXIC EXPOSURES   18

CHAPTER 3: AIR POLLUTANTS   20
Landfills ~ Automobile Emissions ~ Occupational Exposures ~ Second- and Third-Hand Cigarette Smoke

CHAPTER 4: FOODS   27
Preservatives ~ Additives

CHAPTER 5: DRINKING WATER   37

CHAPTER 6: CHEMICAL SUBSTANCES   40
Cigarettes/Recreational Drugs/Alcohol ~ Over-the-Counter and Prescription Medications

CHAPTER 7: PERSONAL CARE PRODUCTS   43

CHAPTER 8: HOUSEHOLD PRODUCTS   50
Cleaning Products ~ Cookware ~ Plastics

CHAPTER 9: RELATIONSHIPS   58
Victim ~ Perpetrator ~ Co-conspirator

SECTION SUMMARY   64

PART 3: DETOXIFICATION PATHWAYS   67

CHAPTER 10: SUPPORTING THE DETOXIFICATION
        PATHWAYS/EMUNCTORIES   69

Kidneys ~ Intestines ~ Lungs ~ Lymphatics ~ Skin ~ Liver ~ Uterus ~ Mind

PART 4 : HOLISTIC DETOXIFICATION STEP BY STEP   77

CHAPTER 11: DETOXIFICATION MEAL TYPES   79

Hypoallergenic/Elimination Diet ~ Modified Fasting ~ Fasting

CHAPTER 12: STRATEGIES FOR SUCCESSFUL
        HOLISTIC DETOXIFICATION   84

Benefits of Detox ~ Strategies before Beginning a Detox ~ Strategies during a Detox ~ Strategies to end Detox Meals ~ Detox Maintenance

CHAPTER 13: SUPPORTIVE DETOXIFICATION THERAPIES   105

Hydrotherapies ~ Castor Oil Packs ~ Complaint Fasting ~ Counseling

CHAPTER 14: DETOX-STYLE   114

Meal Impact Charts ~ Guided Cleansing Timelines

CHAPTER 15: DETOXIFICATION PROTOCOLS   126

Food Consumption list ~ Avoid Foods List ~ Sample Menus ~ Recipes

CONCLUSION   138

AFTERWORD   140

REFERENCES   144

ACKNOWLEDGMENTS   149

ABOUT THE AUTHOR   151

INDEX   152

PREFACE

WHY A HOLISTIC DETOX-STYLE APPROACH?

I DEFINE DETOX-STYLE AS PARTICIPATING IN HABITS AND PRACTICES OF detoxification as a way of life. Detoxification is not merely a periodic necessity but an ongoing practice that should be incorporated into lifestyle changes. Unlike any other detoxification books currently on the market, this book provides a more comprehensive perspective on cleansing. I discuss what it means to holistically release toxins (this includes the body, mind, and spirit) while continuing to support the body's built-in detoxification channels on a regular basis. Health is indeed a journey that will have many detours, side roads, and entrance/exit ramps, along with fast and slow lanes. Unfortunately, there is no final destination to health. It truly is a lifelong process. This means that maintaining it must become a lifestyle practice. With toxins being a continual part of our daily lives, it is imperative that we adopt a Detox-style to eliminate them as frequently as we are exposed to them. The ongoing support of a Detox-style creates a platform for improved health and longevity. While you are traveling along the journey toward an optimal state of wellness, I want to help you make it as fluid a process as possible. This useful guide is designed to serve as an ongoing resource of information for you to cruise along your health journey instead of painfully panting through the path.

Providing a comprehensive perspective on any health and wellness topic that includes a holistic lifestyle approach is of vital significance to you as the reader. As easy as it is to compartmentalize our bodies, it really is one unified whole with different aspects that we refer to as the physical, mental, emotional, and spiritual self. Each aspect of the human body has a unique set of required nourishments that must be fulfilled each day, throughout the day, for optimal function. It is not a one time goal, it is an ongoing process. Whenever one aspect of ourselves is out of balance it creates imbalance in other aspects as well. What begins on the level of spiritual, mental or emotional imbalance or dissatisfaction will over time manifest itself on the level of physical disturbances that, if left unchecked, can cause illness and disease. I can say this based off of not only mind/body science but also what I have seen in the lives of my patients and what I have experienced with my own health.

"Physician heal thyself."
—Luke 4:23 (KJV)

ABOUT THE AUTHOR'S HOLISTIC JOURNEY

I HAVE BEEN LYING

FOR THE PAST FEW YEARS, I HAVE WALKED AROUND LYING TO ALL WHO would listen to me say that going through medical school was the hardest thing I have ever had to do. The rigor of completing seventy-five classes composed of 252 credit hours over a nearly four-and-a-half-year period seemed to be the most daunting task ever. The two brutal years of basic sciences entailed spending what seemed like endless hours in the cadaver lab, touching every inch of the human body while memorizing the names of all structures. Can you even imagine recalling all the nerves, sixty thousand miles of blood vessels, superficial and deep muscles, fascia, ligaments, tendons, origins and insertion points, every aspect of each organ, and every groove, crevice, and orifice of every bone in the human body? Not only did I have to be capable of identifying all of this in less than 60 seconds, my professors had the audacity to ask me to spell it all correctly too.

I mean, do my patients really care if I can spell "spondylolisthesis"? The fact that I can say it without stuttering and know its meaning should be enough proof of my intellect. If you think this is enormous, this only details the *anatomy courses* of the six to eight medical classes I took every trimester for those four rigorous years. Those challenging years seemed endless with exams, practicums, presentations, research papers, clinical hours, countless hours studying and preparing, and not to mention two national board exams. Their ongoing sentiment was that only winners win, so I had a choice of enduring the academic rigor or going home. There were definitely many times I didn't feel confident that I had the fortitude, motivation, and discipline to make it, but I never gave up. After spending years dedicated to making my education the primary focus of my time and attention, I had finally completed all of the classes, clinical training, other necessary requirements, and an abundance of life lessons (for this stage). In an auditorium packed to the gills with people, the name "Dr. Tawainna Houston" was announced as I knelt down to have my doctoral hood placed over my head.

It took all the strength and resilience inside me to get to that moment perceived as the pinnacle of academic achievement. As a result, I naturally thought it was the hardest thing I ever had to do. Throughout those years and even beyond I would repeat over and over again that getting through medical school was the hardest thing I ever had to do; it had became my mantra. Looking back, I now realize it has been a combination of getting to and staying at an ideal weight, not just for months or years, but over a lifetime that has been my most difficult life task thus far. As rigorous as those four years were, medical school does not compare to the lifetime needed to consistently work on mental, emotional, spiritual, and physical balance every moment of every day as a means of staying healthy.

I am a survivor of childhood traumas that include parental absenteeism/abandonment, molestation, and scandal. As a result, one of my coping mechanisms was to develop a protective shield of fat around me to reduce any bad or good attention that I felt I could not handle at that time of my life. Through it all, I perpetuated a deep-seated sense of unworthiness. All of those negative childhood experiences have long since ended, but the residual effects are still encrusted in some of the cracks and crevices of my very being. Therefore, it has taken very intentional effort on my part to stay on a journey of healing instead of a journey focused on victimization or self-defeat.

Some periods of my life have been more challenging than others as I worked toward my healing. Thankfully, some moments have been a bit more graceful. This fluctuation in the healing process, coupled with the basic unfolding of regular life challenges, has also directly correlated with challenges with maintaining my ideal weight. This is far from an excuse for being an overweight naturopathic doctor. Instead, it is a disclosure of transparency between me as the expert—my education, knowledge, and continual practice—and you as the reader that will help you learn from not only the resources I provide, but my life experiences as well.

Instead of waiting until I have perfected what it means to completely break through trauma and live a perfectly balanced life of health and wholeness, I decided to invite you along on my journey as it continues to unfold. You will have a doctor currently living and growing through the process with you providing honesty about the difficulties of balancing whole health and life, especially when there is a history of trauma involved.

I have decades of experience with weight gain and weight loss as I managed the physical manifestation of what was rooted in the mental and emotional traumas of my childhood. Although I sought out counseling as an adult for my childhood traumas and depression, it was not until my early thirties that I began to understand that my weight gain and emotional issues were not separate events that needed to be compartmentalized. Rather, they were deeply intertwined and had to be managed first at the root level.

As much as it may be needed by you, you will be hard-pressed to find a doctor who will write you a prescription for self-love before she writes you a prescription for the latest weight loss drug. Learning to love yourself, flaws and all, just won't happen as fast as popping a few appetite suppressants to lose those extra twenty pounds before your cousin's wedding next month or your upcoming class reunion.

What I have learned is that until you address problems from the root, the issue never completely heals. Unfortunately, after the pills, the diets, or the bariatric surgery, most patients gain weight back if portion control is not the root of the issue. From the time I was about eight years old until today, I have not been at my ideal weight for more than two weeks at a time. With each successful natural weight loss—twenty-five or fifty or eighty pounds or my highest net weight loss of 121 pounds—I have only been able to linger briefly around what science says is my ideal weight before my body gradually began to increase and stabilize, usually with an increase of fifteen to twenty pounds. This stabilization only occurs if all the other aspects of my life are balanced at that time. Not feeling sad has been important; otherwise, it usually feels as though I have to fight or at least arm wrestle every day to avoid numbing my pain with sugar, which converts to pounds and eventually turns into more pain.

Richard Bach once said, "You teach best what you most need to learn."[1] This is the most accurate statement that parallels my whole-hearted passion for guiding others to a better quality of life via optimized health and wellness with my lifelong struggle to be fully free of my past traumas. Henri Nowen[2] might refer to me as a "wounded healer" because my passion to heal others is what keeps me actively participating in my own healing journey. As my healing process continues to unfold, I have come to accept my perfect imperfections. I am not at all happy with being at any weight that exceeds my ability to move freely, fluidly, and without weight-bearing pain. Doing so negates my health belief system, is downright uncomfortable, and unacceptable. I have come to accept that because of my history of trauma and longstanding emotional issues that derived from it have caused my journey of health and wellness to require significantly more intentional effort than that of someone without a history of trauma. One person's additional 30 percent commitment to a healthy lifestyle of emotional balance, healthier eating, and exercising more may help them lose weight. My equivalent to that is a need for a consistent 85 percent minimum dedication to self-expression and fulfill-

---

1   Richard Bach, from *Illusions: the Adventures of a Reluctant Messiah* (Toronto: Delacorte Press, 1978).

ment, stress management, restful sleep, healthy eating, and exercising just to maintain at my current weight.

I can honestly say that I am intentional every day about providing more health-restorative foods and lifestyle behaviors to my body than exposing it to many of the toxic factors that will deteriorate it. Nonetheless, the effort required for me to stay balanced still remains considerably higher because I am working against the resistance of old negative mental tapes in my head. In addition, there are also the biochemical changes from a lifetime of weight fluctuations that has contributed to a slower metabolism and smaller yet increased number of fat cells present in my body that want to be fed. These fat cells can grow back into a state of greater obesity if left unchecked. This lends credence to why a Detox-style plays such a significant role in not only preventing disease but helping to manage it. Getting to the goal of losing weight is one thing, but it is maintaining the body at any level and improving it even further that requires an ongoing lifestyle change by controlling toxic factors. This can be done by adopting a Detox-style.

My call to service to help others with their health journeys keeps me empowered enough to stay on my personal wellness horse that during my darkest hours of life seems more like a raging bull trying to buck me off. However, each time I fall down, I remember all the instructions and prescriptions I have given to countless patients and others. I muster up the strength and fortitude required to get back up again. Even though it has happened in the past, a twenty-pound weight gain does not have to turn into a fifty-pound weight gain. This could easily happen if I decide to stay down instead of wiping off the dust of my shame and embarrassment and once again straddle my wellness horse to continue my trot toward wellness.

With every patient that I help, I am helping myself as well. This is what wounded healers do. What is outlined in this book in not coming from a doctor simply providing statistics, science, and therapies that have enhanced the health and well-being of others. Instead they have been an integral part of my own personal journey of wellness. Staying on the straight and narrow over the course of an entire lifetime sounds great in theory, but I know firsthand that consistently maintaining a Detox-style is and will be the ultimate challenge for many others and me. It is definitely worth the daily effort.

---

2   Henri Nouwen, The Wounded Healer (New York: Doubleday, 1972).

JOURNEY OF WELLNESS

I named my practice *Journey of Wellness Natural Medicine Center* instead of *Journey to Wellness* because I realized in that moment that you never really reach that destination since holistic wellness is not a linear process. Life and our bodies change from the moment we are born until the moment we die: our bodies grow and develop while we are young and still coming into an awareness of who we really are. This occurs while we are dependent upon our caretakers to provide us with the necessary resources to maintain our health where food, nurturing, and safety are concerned. As young adults we experience life and make more independent decisions while emotions swing like a pendulum from one end to the other. We eat socially (or not), and practice risky behaviors that can impact our health. Young adults also face pregnancy, changing roles and new responsibilities. Middle-agers contend with maturing bodies, family obligations, financial issues, and occupational shifts, so getting to a place of balance, stability, and better time management seems to be a perpetual dream. During old age, seniors are facing similar issues as the middle-agers, but they have more free-time (if retired) and usually lower quality of life because of their frequent doctors' visits due to a declining health status.

As life changes, so does our ability to stay balanced and evenly distribute our time, energy, and focus on all the aspects of life and the people who matter. It is these demands on our time, energy, and focus that make it easier to put our health on the back burner until it is absolutely necessary to pay closer attention to it on a more consistent basis. Sometimes there are those welcomed seasons throughout life when the primary aspects of life seem stable enough that health is made an intentional daily priority for those who value good health. This involves incorporating a variety of good habits into your daily lifestyle and staying disciplined. When emergencies like unfortunate, unplanned, and certainly unwelcome events occur in life, discipline and focus on health will oftentimes get shifted. "Shifted" does not mean disregarded because they are habits now being shared with new life events that need to be managed.

Here in America, it requires some level of commitment, energy, and focus to practice health disciplines that are not supported as the norm. This is why *intentionality* becomes important. You must make a conscious daily effort to choose a Detox-style, such as the recommendations outlined in the upcoming chapters of this book instead of accepting the readily accessible unhealthy options received by the masses. It does not take much for life to tug you in such a way that the health disciplines you had maintained for the previous three months or year have been reduced by 35 to 80 percent. This can easily occur due to a new stressful situation at your job or in your relationships, your child's new extracurricular activities that completely change your schedule, the passing of someone you love, or a traumatic event from the past that crept back up. Even with the best health intentions, your time, energy, and focus get shifted. All of these situations are a continual part of life. Over time, we will all learn to balance, but some of us may have to do it a thousand times. Although life changes, we must stay engaged in wellness habits such as a Detox-style that will prevent disease.

The purpose of incorporating a Detox-style on this journey of wellness is to recondition ourselves to eventually make cleansing our internal body a subconscious habit. Whether you are dealing with issues of weight, allergies, chronic diseases, autoimmune disease, or any other health conditions you will benefit from supporting your body's ability to be healthy by reducing your toxic load.

There are a variety of elements that we are exposed to every day that diminish our quality of life. Adopting a Detox-style is the best way to eliminate or significantly reduce the role that toxic buildup has contributed toward our health imbalance. Taking a holistic approach to detoxification will ensure that your health and well-being are optimized and not simply managed. As I have already demonstrated here, imbalance in any aspect of health will negatively impact other aspects of health. It becomes vital to participate regularly in practices conducive to creating an internal environment for ourselves that is holistically life supporting more often than it is life taking. I now invite you to join the journey of wellness with me by adopting a Detox-style.

DEDICATION

THIS BOOK IS DEDICATED TO MS. ZANDI K. FENNELL (1975–2011), MY Howard University Sistah and my Sistah in Natural Medicine. Although God called you home much earlier than any of us expected, your passion for people, health, and healing the planet lives on in me and in the many lives that you touched during your journey on this earthly realm. May you eternally rest in peace, my Soul Sistah!

WHO SHOULD READ THIS BOOK?

If you have **allergies,** this book will expose you to potential toxins that are causing you to remain reactive to potential allergens.

If you have any **autoimmune diseases** such as **lupus, celiac disease, multiple sclerosis, Hashimotos thyroiditis, rheumatoid arthritis** or others, the information in this book will help you strengthen your body to naturally manage your condition and reduce your symptoms.

If you have any **chronic diseases,** such as **hypertension, heart disease, diabetes, high cholesterol, gout, arthritis, endocrine disorders**, or others, following the tips on the following pages to support your detoxification pathways will significantly improve your condition naturally.

If you are **infertile,** this book will help elevate your awareness of some of the toxins to which you can reduce your exposure and naturally support your body's ability to reproduce by improving your health.

If you are a **pregnant woman or parent,** this book will help you support the healthy growth and development of your fetus and children by reducing their exposure to controllable toxins.

If you have **skin conditions,** this book will provide you with the information to move the toxins out of your body so that the improvement in your health will become evident in your newly glowing skin.

If you want a healthy jump start to your **weight loss** program, then this book gives you the tools to help mobilize toxins to move out of your body so you can shed those pounds more easily.

If you have **fibroids, polycystic ovarian syndrome (PCOS), breast cancer, menopause complications, or other women's health conditions,** this book will identify the most common toxic exposures that disrupt hormones and the impact they have on your health and well-being.

If you have a job at a **fire department, hair/nail salon, industrial plant, manufacturing warehouses, work as a professional driver,** and a long list of other occupations that expose you to a variety of environmental and occupational toxins, this book will assist you with natural ways to keep your job from adding to the deterioration of your health.

INTRODUCTION

I GREW UP IN A BLUE COLLAR FAMILY WITH MANY OF MY RELATIVES WORK-
ing for the local automobile plant in our small town. After spending
an eight-to-twelve-hour workday on an assembly line, it was not unusual for them to end their day, especially if it was a Friday (payday), with
some savory barbecue rib tips and fries or a large steak and cheese sub
from some of the local eateries that were still open at one and two a.m.
Every bite of their saucy, cheesy, mouth-watering meals felt rewarding
after completing the laborious tasks of assembling motor vehicle parts. A
fat paycheck in hand and a belly full of good tasting food felt like a slice of
heaven as they showered and prepared to go into a coma-like sleep from
all that heavy food and fatigue. This was a regular routine for many au-
tomotive plant workers in my town. Unfortunately, a lifelong history of
poor lifestyle and dietary habits has a way of accumulating into multiple
health problems.

My relatives and so many others like them who spend decades working in various types of factories, warehouses, and industrial plants are on
the front lines and have numerous toxic exposures being dumped into
their bodies every day due to their occupational environments. When
you factor in ongoing dietary choices that include foods high in toxic additives and preservatives, this becomes a disastrous recipe that does not
end favorably.

Toxins are ubiquitous: they are everywhere and there is absolutely no
escaping contact with them. Each day we dump an enormous amount
of toxins into our bodies simply through living. Toxins are in the air we
breathe, the food we eat, the water we drink, our household supplies, our
personal hygiene products, our environment, and our relationships. The
amount of exposure can be controlled to some degree, but in some cases

(such as air) it just is, unless you want to wait until you arrive somewhere safer to resume breathing. Good luck with that. The possibility of escaping toxins does not exist, but we can do what is necessary to reduce our exposure and cleanse our bodies of unnecessary waste materials on a regular basis via adopting a Detox-style.

Unfortunately, in American society the problem and the solution are on different sides of the same coin, which is detoxification pathways. If the coin itself is detoxification pathways on one side, Americans are blocking up the detoxification channels, which is destructive to our health. On the other side of the coin, if we can increase function or support of the detoxification pathways in our bodies it will significantly improve our health and well-being. Let's admit it, some jobs, like truck driving, are simply not conducive to taking regular bathroom breaks. The kidneys are a detoxification pathway that release waste products via urine, but if you are not excreting urine because of lack of hydration out of concern for not wanting to stop and urinate—or any other reason for that matter, those toxins are not being eliminated. Wearing an antiperspirant will help us look cool and calm during a job interview or presentation in front of a large crowd, but those are not life events that would justify daily blocking our sweat glands, which is another detoxification pathway. Then there is the most significant elimination channel in the body, the colon. The colon does not get used nearly as often as it should even in the people who consider themselves to be "healthy." I have found that this organ system gets underutilized for a variety of reasons that oftentimes lead back to a lack of understanding of the purpose of elimination.

Over the years, I have experienced countless encounters with patients and people in general who are embarrassed by their poop, embarrassed to talk about or look at their poop after they have finished eliminating. Given the chance some would just rather not have one because that is just how disgusting they think their own bowel movements are. One of my medical school professors once shared a story with my class about a med student who admitted that she had never seen her own poop before because it was too gross. And to think she was an aspiring doctor. I must admit the aroma of a full bowel movement in the average person is usually not pleasant and depending on the meal you are eliminating it can at times be downright awful. Nonetheless, if it smells that bad on the outside of your body, imagine the damage it is doing by lingering around inside your body for too long. What if it never fully came out at all? Fecal matter is a complete waste product that is filled with bacteria and toxins that needs to be eliminated from the body as quickly as possible. The longer it stays inside, the more damage is does over time. It is the cumulative impact of this type of toxic build up and more that I will be discussing in this book.

When we accumulate trash in our homes, we take it out to the curbside for the neighborhood sanitation to pick up and dispose. The trash is overflowing with food products such as fat or the skin of meats, raw fleshy meats, fresh produce, and other leftover meals dumped into the wastebasket, an odor consumes the house if the trash is not removed quickly. Imagine those same foods in a house with no air conditioner on a day that it is ninety-eight degrees outside. The stench will hit you before you can open the door all the way. The internal temperature of a human body is approximately 98.6 degrees Fahrenheit; therefore, waste products that sit around inside our bodies are putrefying, fermenting, and becoming rotten from all the heat and moisture. The only difference between what is happening with waste inside our hot homes versus inside of our hot bodies is that the smell is direct, the flies are visible, and the maggots are tangible, so we must get the trash out quickly. It is just as urgent inside of our waste-filled bodies. If we are only having a bowel movement once a day or a few times a week, the bacteria-filled waste material is not coming out as quickly or as often as it needs to.

For so long, bowel movements have been a TMI (too much information) matter even when talking to physicians. However, I am a naturopathic doctor and, for me, knowing full details of the characteristics of my patients' bowel movements is a very important component to understanding their health. I ask patients to get as descriptive about it as possible from color, length, shape, fullness, odor, additional particles in their waste such as blood, mucus, or undigested food, as well as how difficult or easy it is to eliminate. If you are frowning up now, I may not be the doctor for you, but hopefully by the end of this book you will change your mind. Understanding bowel characteristics provides me with a more in-depth clinical picture of potential health disturbances. As you read through the book, you will have a better understanding of all the toxins that we encounter on a regular basis and the impact they have on the body. One of the most effective ways to manage, reduce, or reverse the disease process (if possible), is to regularly detoxify by incorporating a Detox-style to give the body the support it needs to continue to be a self-healing, self-repairing, self-regenerating organism. Maintaining good bowel habits is an imperative part of the process of supporting great natural health.

"Take care of your body, it's the only place you have to live."
—Jim Rohn

PART I

CUMULATIVE TOXIC EXPOSURES AND ITS IMPACT ON HEALTH

CHAPTER 1

CONTROLLING DISEASE VS. PROMOTING HEALTH

TOXINS DEFINED

THE UNITED STATES NATIONAL LIBRARY OF MEDICINE DEFINES TOXins as substances created by plants and animals that are poisonous to humans. Toxins can also include metals such as lead and mercury as well as to medications.

The term *toxins,* as referenced in this book, will be defined as any physical, chemical, or energetic particles that make contact with human beings in small or large amounts and slow down, stop, negatively alter, or reverse normal cellular processes, growth, and development.

THE WORLD HEALTH ORGANIZATION

In 1948, the World Health Organization (WHO) developed a definition of what health is and defined it as "health is a state of physical, mental, and social well-being and not merely the absence of disease or infirmity.¹" WHO is the most influential reference point for management of public health care standards; they develop the gold standard for disease prevention, immunizations, disease testing, and disease management protocols. So much about life and the status of one's health has changed tremendously since this definition was implemented in 1948 as

---

1   WHO Definition of Health. (1948, April 7) Retrieved from http://www.who.int/about/definition/en/print.html

part of the WHO constitution, the foundational principle is needed even more strongly today than it may have been during the establishment of the definition. In spite of great advancements of technology, the rate at which Americans, in particular, are developing life-threatening and chronic diseases is increasing rapidly. Standards of protocol have been implemented for early detection of diseases, an increasing amount of new pharmaceutical drugs, new surgical devices and techniques. While these measures manage and control diseases, a more effective measure to promote health would be disease prevention. Allocating hundreds of millions of dollars for educating the general public about the importance of mammograms, prostate exams, and colonoscopies for the purpose of early detection of cancer cell growth is not the same as spending hundreds of millions of dollars on educating the masses on methods to prevent cancer cell growth within the body. Therefore, health is being addressed from a perspective of disease management instead of wellness care.

With all the various diagnostic lab testing and imaging available, it is evident that disease diagnosis and management have taken the leading role in health. Prevention and the "whole health" component of the WHO's definition of health has been left out of the current medical model, thus leaving society at an extreme disadvantage. This is demonstrated by present-day morbidity (living in a diseased state of being) and mortality (number of deaths) rates from preventable disease such as heart disease and cancer which cause well over a million deaths annually.[3] Because conventional medicine has become so disease management driven, it misconstrues the view of what health truly is. As a result, I believe that the WHO should be the foundation for discussing Detox-style.

WHO's definition quickly dismisses the assumption that many people easily make and that is, if they have not been given a disease diagnosis they are healthy. This perception is inaccurate, because many people are usually not paying attention to subtle changes in the body's fatigue, digestive patterns, and mobility adjustments. The mental and emotional components, particularly, get overlooked because many people are stressed in one way or another. Therefore, they tend to participate in various unhealthy coping mechanisms that help numb their feelings. These activities become second nature to the perpetual engagement of stressful triggers.

No one is exempt from some level of stress, but not many will understand that they are unhealthy because of it. It can often take some extended time before signs and symptoms are presenting strong enough for people to begin to pay attention and seek medical care. The body deteriorates over time, but we control the slope of the rate at which that happens.

Chapter 1: Controlling Disease vs. Promoting Health

I have had a plethora of patients say to me, "Dr. Houston, since I have turned forty [or fifty or sixty], my body just seems to be falling apart. Everything hurts all the time and things just don't seem the same." Disease-free is not the same as being healthy. I gently help them understand that it is not simply chronological age that is causing their bodies to present ailments. Indeed, a natural decline in hormones and decades of physical, mental, and emotional wear and tear have all contributed to deterioration of the body is to be expected. Nonetheless, it is a combination of the natural deterioration of the body, the lifetime culmination of dietary and lifestyle factors, and other toxic exposures that can contribute to a forty-year-old patient internally aging more rapidly that causes her to feel decades older.

The disease process did not just begin at the onset of your first symptom. Instead, the symptom was merely an indicator to bring your awareness to something being present at a stage where it is now possibly detectable. With many disease processes such as heart disease or cancer, these conditions exist for sometimes twenty years or longer before they develop to the point of being symptomatic or detectable by basic lab tests or imaging scans. It is the onset of these symptoms that causes patients to seek out further evaluation.

Health is something we are either building, maintaining, or destroying every day through our dietary lifestyles, behaviors, attitudes, and exposures. Over a course of one's lifetime, the cumulative effect of the different variables will speed up the process of the natural deterioration of the human body or slow down that same decline. The more life-supporting behaviors you practice, the longer your body will feel supported in the process of thriving instead of simply surviving. Obtaining kidney dialysis three times per week will help you survive longer, but thriving at optimal levels becomes more challenging when so much of your time and energy is being devoted to simply staying alive, due to the length of time involved in each treatment and associated fatigue.

As the true definition of health, as defined by the WHO, is considered, it is important for you to understand that positively contributing to your health on a daily basis is what helps you retain a healthy state of being at any age. Although a disease may not be present, engaging in more life-destructive behaviors, such as poor dietary and lifestyle habits, is contributing to the development of disease. These behaviors encourage a toxic breeding ground within the body. As discussed throughout this book, toxins are a reoccurring part of our daily lives. Unless we can survive off of air alone in a pure oxygen-filled bubble, we will always be exposed to toxins. The good news is that by adopting a Detox-style, we can choose to limit our controllable factors and/or become intentional about supporting the detoxification pathways that are within our bodies. They are designed to continually eliminate waste products, but often go unsupported. The exposure to toxins alone is not killing us; it is combined with the culmination of our daily choices. Every day we are either slowing down or speeding up an accumulation of insulting factors that over time can manifest into a disease process within the body.

CUMULATIVE EFFECT OF TOXINS

Due to the ubiquitous nature of toxins, it does not require much life interaction for exposure levels to quickly accumulate. Unless you are a person with asthma or allergies, you will not usually feel the immediate impact of the cellular damage of toxins in your body because it is a slow developing process that builds up over time. It is important to note that the rate of toxic buildup in the body increases with higher daily exposures to toxins. Internal toxic waste buildup is exponentially increased by participation in substandard dietary and lifestyle behaviors. As toxins continue to build up without being released from the body, the natural flow of cellular processes within the body are slowly altered over time.

For instance, let's compare your daily accumulation of toxic exposures to the mess in your kitchen after your family of eight has finished cooking and eating Thanksgiving dinner. There is a pile of pots and pans and other dishes that need to be washed and tons of leftover food that needs to be stored away. The kitchen floor is filled with bread crumbs, gravy stains, and minced veggies that need to be swept and mopped. The appliances and counters have cheese sauce clumps, melted butter, and salad dressing smeared over them and they need to be wiped down. There are food cans and boxes, plastic wrap, aluminum foil, and uneaten food on the kids' plates that all need to be discarded in the already overflowing trash can that needs to be emptied into a larger container prepared for sanitation pickup. The natural inclination is to eliminate that entire mess so that the kitchen looks and smells fresh and clean. Instead of cleaning up, the entire family leaves to catch the Black Friday sales that start on Thursday evening. After arriving home at two in the morning, they all decide to eat again and go to bed. This cycle continues for the following week and no one lifts a finger to clean anything but they all have significantly added to the original mess. After a week, the house is unsightly and the stench from the trash and spoiled food is deplorable. Just as this household mess in just a one week time can quickly build up, the same is true for the human body.

With weeklong neglect of this kitchen, the smell will draw unwanted pests, the overflowing trash is obstructing the walkway and the floor is sticky. You can't get water from the sink because all the dishes are piled up and blocking the movement of the faucet. There is no room on the countertops or stove tops to sit anything down because the holiday meal leftovers have never been stored away. You can't cook any new meals because there is simply no room in the kitchen to use it as it was designed.

The resources needed to get the kitchen clean are still operable: the faucet still runs water, the garbage disposal still works, the dishwasher works, and the sanitation person still comes once or twice per week to collect garbage. The problem is that the channels to get the house clean are not being utilized so that it can support the cleaning process. Cleaning this kitchen and keeping it cleaned on a regular basis requires intentionality from the family that lives there and uses it every day. The flow of cooking and cleaning has been disrupted by this growing mess that has gotten out of control.

Similar to the kitchen, a disruption to the natural flow of cellular processes will ultimately disturb the natural function of the organs and organ systems. The inability of the organs and organ systems to perform their jobs effectively produces a need for other interventions. As a naturopathic doctor, I would do a thorough evaluation of the full clinical picture of the patient to understand all factors contributing to their organ system disturbances. It is my goal to enhance organ function by removing all perceived barriers and blockages that are impeding the natural process. This could include removing toxins, modifying diet and lifestyle factors, addressing nutritional deficiencies, strengthening and tonifying the organs with herbal supplementation, and wellness counseling. This natural way of eliminating the cumulative effects of toxins and restoring function is done by simply providing the body with the resources it needs to function as it was naturally designed by surviving and thriving.

Unfortunately, naturopathic medicine is not the primary course of action for the average American when medical interventions are needed. Pharmaceutical drugs and surgery are usually the "gold standard" of medical treatment whenever the body is demonstrating signs and symptoms of being out of balance. Sadly, in many cases the medications and surgeries are doing more to suppress or manipulate function than to support the already built-in self-repair mechanisms of the body. While these techniques are definitely needed in acute emergency situations or life-threatening disease, this level of intervention is not always required for other standard or chronic conditions. Suppression and manipulation of function is a significant contributing factor to the plethora of side effects that can follow treatment. The body is an interconnected organism that can be impacted in seemingly unrelated areas by altering, suppressing, or replacing function in one area. This can disturb your overall sense of well-being.

In reference to the kitchen example, conventional medicine would begin with addressing the symptoms of the uncleanliness. Air freshener would be sprayed throughout the kitchen to mask the smell. Pest control products will be used to temporarily eliminate all the flies, roaches, ants, and other bugs swarming around. Soon the foul odor returns and is permeating the entire house. The pests have increased in number and the new, extra-strength products don't seem to be effective. Surgery is required to remove the back door to the kitchen for a continual surge of fresh air and an exit for the pests. The side effect is that now more pests are entering the kitchen from the outdoors than leaving the kitchen, all of the fresh air is causing the house to become cold, and the utility bill has increased by 40 percent. The surgeons return to attach a door that has a glass on top and a screen at the bottom to create a minimized version of fresh air circulation. It also has a detachable shield to cover the screen whenever the temperature is discomforting. The residents continue to spray the heavy duty, industrial-strength pest control that won't remove the pests, but may keep their numbers from growing.

My holistic, naturopathic approach would be to sit down with the parents long enough to find out why they have an odor and pest control problem in the kitchen. I would then directly inquire about any lifestyle factors and possible mental or emotional issues that have caused the whole family to neglect cleaning up their kitchen for an entire week, especially after a huge holiday meal. At the top of their wellness plan list would be taking out all that trash (toxins) to ensure that people can move around the kitchen unobstructed. We would then establish an efficient way to cleanse and deodorize the entire kitchen to improve its safety, appearance, and usage. The kitchen, in most homes, is in frequent use throughout the day, not unlike our bodies' exposure to toxins. Therefore keeping it cleaned after each meal, or at the very least at the end of each day, keeps the mess (toxins) from accumulating to the point of showing signs and symptoms of uncleanliness.

As you can see, a one-meal mess or a few toxins, if left unchecked, can quickly snowball into a more serious condition over time. You are exposed to toxins daily and supporting the natural detoxification pathways in the body helps reduce the cumulative buildup of insulting factors that can lead to a disturbance or chronic imbalance in health. This type of ongoing stress on the organs can produce signs and symptoms that show up as a toxic presentation, which can include the following:

Toxic Presentation in the Body

- Acne

- Allergies

- Asthma

- Autoimmune Diseases

- Brain Fog

- Chemical Sensitivity

- Depression

- Diabetes

- Fatigue

- Headaches

- Infertility

- Low Libido

- Mood Swings

- Obesity

- Temperature Problems

When toxins build up in the body over extended periods of time because they are not being released through the proper detoxification channels, they begin to manifest through many of the presentations listed above. These presentations may be individualized or a collection of many different symptoms and will often be named a particular disease according to the organ or organ system it is impacting.

TOXIC IMPACT ON ORGAN SYSTEMS

As you read the pages ahead regarding various toxic exposures and their impact on different organ systems, the list below provides you with more specific diseased conditions that the toxins can cause to that area of the body.

1. Nervous System (Neurotoxic)
    —Multiple Sclerosis, Alzheimer's, Parkinson's disease, memory decline

2. Immune System (Immunotoxic)
    —Allergies, autoimmune conditions, chronic fatigue, viral infections

3. Endocrine System (Endocrine Disruptors, those which interfere with hormone function)
    —Thyroid, adrenals, male and female fertility, endocrine-related cancers, diabetes

4. Cardiovascular System (Cardiotoxic)
    —Heart disease, atherosclerosis, stroke, high blood pressure

5. Cancers
    —Varying types induced by toxic exposure and can cause cell proliferation (increase)

CHAPTER 2

TOXIC BUILDUP AND ITS THREAT TO THE FAMILY

ENDOCRINE DISRUPTORS

THE ROLE OF TOXINS IN THE EVERYDAY LIFE OF A FAMILY HAS A HUGE impact for everyone involved over time. Individually, most people's health is going to respond a bit differently to toxic exposure; however, in the case of the family, variable factors are determined mostly by age and sex. Although there are a multitude of toxins crossing your daily path, it is the toxic chemicals that cause endocrine disruption that have far-reaching effects. Endocrine disruptors not only impact an individual's health reaction to toxic exposure but it can also negatively impact reproductive organs, fertility, and fetal development, all of which can affect future generations of offsprings for the family and population growth for society at large.

The endocrine system produces hormones that act as chemical messengers traveling throughout the body via the bloodstream, carrying signals to various organs and tissues. These hormonal signals participate in the coordination of complex processes that includes sex, reproduction, growth, and metabolism, in addition to altering mood and behavior. The body relies on the proper balance of these hormones to turn on and off cell signals that keep the body functioning at optimal levels. Endocrine system glands respond to cell signals from the brain for the hormones to be directly secreted into the body by the same glands that produce and store the hormones. Toxic chemicals can mimic the real hormone, causing the body to respond to a falsified signal, thereby interfering with the natural function of the real hormone. This disrupts the endocrine system.

To provide an example of what I mean, let's say you are a parent and you instruct your child that he or she can only open the door for his or her grandparents. If a stranger, who looks identical to the grandparents, shows up the child is going to let them in because that is what he or she has been instructed to do. Once inside the stranger will disrupt the safe environment for the child because the conditions of the home are now being violated by someone the child does not know but has allowed into the home based on a false identity.

COMMON CHEMICALS THAT DISRUPT THE ENDOCRINE SYSTEM

This following list of toxins and the products in which endocrine disruptors can be found is NOT exhaustive and should only be used as a reference to common exposures.

- **Dioxins**—found in dairy products

- **Pesticides**—found in foods

- **Polychlorinated Biphenyls (PCBs)**—found in fish, meat, and dairy products

- **Phthalates**—found in plastics (bottles, wraps, containers, bags), cosmetics, nail polish

- **Parabens**—found in lotions, shampoos, soaps

- **Bisphenol-A (BPA)**—found in plastics

- **Volatile Solvents**—found in gasoline, exhaust fumes, grease cleaners, paints, nail polish, nail polish removers, adhesives, glues, printing inks

- **Formaldehyde**—found in off gassing of new furniture and carpets

- **Heavy Metals**—such as lead, cadmium, mercury

EMBRYO/FETUS/INFANTS/CHILDREN

EMBRYO/FETUS

During the very early stages of embryonic development the cells are dividing, replicating, and differentiating, which means the cells are multiplying in number and becoming more specialized to play their specific roles within the body. This process continues to take place on a larger scale as the embryo develops into a fetus with more identifiable physical traits like hands, fingers, legs, and such. Throughout this time of development from conception to birth, there are toxic exposures that cross the placental barrier that can impact the health of the unborn. Toxins can adversely impact the biochemical function of cells throughout the fetal organ system, in addition to structural development, all of which can negatively impact health outcomes. The risk of poor health outcomes are variable and include factors such as the amount and type of toxic exposures, the stage of pregnancy, and the metabolic rate of the mother. Negative health outcomes that can arise from ongoing toxic exposures can include but are not limited to: miscarriages, premature births, low birth weights, congenital anomalies, and neurodevelopment problems. Other birth defects can include sexual organ malformations and gender development that arises from toxic chemicals that cause endocrine disruption. Ultimately, there is a direct correlation between the health of the mother prior to conception, during pregnancy, and after delivery and the health of her offspring throughout all stages of development.

An abbreviated list of Common Toxins and associated adverse health outcomes include:

Arsenic	Low birth weight, fetal malformation, fetal death, spontaneous abortion, stillbirth and preterm births
Dioxin	Abnormal embryo development, spontaneous abortion, retardation, feminization, decreased sperm quality, central nervous system malformations
Lead	Neural tube defects, cardiac defects, neurobehavioral problems, hypospadias (male genital defect)
Mercury	Neural tube defects, neurobehavioral problems
Phthalates	Hypospadias (male genital defect)

| **Pesticides** | Low birth weight, congenital anomalies |
| **Tobacco** | Low birth weight, attention deficit hyperactivity disorder |

RECOMMENDATIONS

Unfortunately, the embryological stage of the pregnancy is happening during a time when the average woman is not even aware that she is pregnant yet. Maintaining a healthy body and detoxing on a regular basis for yourself should be standard protocol, and if you unknowingly become pregnant the embryo is growing in an environment pre-established for a healthier outcome. If you are intentionally trying to get pregnant, eliminate the controllable toxic factors that can be contributing to your fertility process. Develop new or additional health behaviors that support your wellness so that you cannot only get pregnant but sustain a healthy body throughout full-term delivery and beyond.

INFANTS/CHILDREN

Infants and children have underdeveloped brains, organs, and organ systems that do not reach maturity until adulthood—two decades past conception. During this time of growth, it is the immaturity of their physical and biochemical makeup that significantly increases their susceptibility to toxic exposure in comparison to adults. Infants and children are consuming more foods and beverages throughout the day, in addition to taking in more air due to their higher resting respiratory rate, which is twice that of adults. The most basic requirements of tasks that include meals, hydration, and breathing alone escalates their potential for encounters with toxic chemicals, not to mention other common daily exposures. Infants and young children have a constant hand-to-mouth contact and mouth-to-everything possible contact—playing with plastic toys, playing on the floor and the ground outdoors—all of which are breeding grounds for a plethora of environmental toxic exposures that can seep in through their highly absorptive skin.

These repetitive exposures, along with so many unmentioned others coming into contact with the vulnerable bodies of infants and children at such a critical time in their development, can accumulate into severe health consequences. Common toxic exposures among infants and children have contributed to adverse health effects that include but are not limited to: developmental disorders, learning disabilities, asthma, allergens, attention deficit disorder (ADD), attention deficit hyperactivity disorder (ADHD), and failure to thrive. In addition to these health complications, repetitive exposure to these toxins as children are developing can compromise their health as adults and make them more susceptible to other chronic diseases and conditions.

Recommendations:
1. Breast-feeding remains the superior form of nutrition for newborns and infants, therefore mom should be consuming healthy organic foods that have not been packaged and processed. Developing these habits early will make it easier to pass on to your children as you prepare them healthy meals and beverages that are contributing to their thriving, growth, and development.

2. Continue to let children run, play, and explore all that the environment has to offer while continuing to supervise and eliminate mouth contact with anything other than food and drinks as much as possible (this is definitely a hard one).

3. Make mindful purchasing choices when choosing plastic toys, accessories, and personal care products to ensure they are free of harmful toxic chemicals.

4. Remove children's shoes and clothing immediately when coming indoors from playing so that outdoor contaminates are not spread throughout the home. This also sounds like a good time to give them a bath.

5. Find other toxic specific recommendations to help you and your children thrive in part two of this book.

WOMEN'S HEALTH

The ability to create, develop, and give birth to a child places a woman's body in a precarious position throughout her lifetime. As beautiful and joyous as the excitement and anticipation is around delivering a child into the world, the entire process from start to finish and even beyond will take a considerable toll on the health of a woman physically, mentally, and spiritually. For most women, life as they once knew it changes in a blink of an eye. Whether it is when they have urinated on the third at-home pregnancy test stick and it still says "positive," the first ultrasound, the first kick, or the newborn's first cry, life changes. Unfortunately, so does a woman's body. However, whether you have children or not, just the simple fact that women are created with the capacity to reproduce makes them susceptible to a variety of other hormonal-related health challenges. An accumulation of toxins, especially those that have been identified as endocrine disruptors, have contributed to hormonal disturbances with a multitude of symptoms and health conditions.

INFERTILITY

Endocrine disruptors can effect hormonal concentrations, reproduction, and block ovulation. Each aspect of the reproductive cycle is driven by a fluctuation of various hormones that are increasing and decreasing at programmed times to release the egg, enable fertilization, or shed the endometrial lining (menses) if no egg has been implanted in the uterus. An accumulation of toxic endocrine disruptors can intercept an egg being fertilized by blocking ovulation from taking place. It also disturbs the natural flow or rhythm when the chemicals mimicking estrogen are in higher concentrations at times when this hormone should be in lower concentrations, which then alters the estrogen/progesterone ratio. These two primary hormones work in concert with each other, circulating with progesterone in lower concentrations during the first fourteen days of a menstrual cycle while the estrogen is more dominant. Regarding fertility, an example would be an unsustainable pregnancy (miscarriage) due to high estrogen levels and low circulating levels of progesterone, which should be the dominant hormone circulating after ovulation to protect embryo implantation.

FIBROID TUMORS AND OTHER WOMEN'S HEALTH CONDITIONS

Fibroids is another condition driven by hormone domination, more specifically estrogen. The body is not only producing its own (endogenous) estrogens that are in circulation but the individual is also coming into contact with (exogenous/synthetic) estrogens made from sources outside the body. These estrogen-like compounds are typically found in processed soy products along with endocrine disruptors found in personal care products and plastics. The cumulative impact of these toxic chemicals causes them to bind to the hormone receptor, which can increase estrogen activity. The excess estrogen is serving as a life line to these (usually) benign uterine tumors that will continue to grow from its estrogen-rich blood supply. Adipose (fat) tissue also serves as a store-house for estrogens; therefore, carrying excess body weight increases estrogen levels within the body.

In addition to infertility and fibroids, toxic buildup can contribute to other common women's health conditions such as: polycystic ovarian syndrome (PCOS), breast cancer, endometriosis, and menopause complications. The key to prevention and/or disease management in these conditions is to minimize toxic exposures in addition to adopting regular detox practices. Later, in chapter 11, you will learn more about detoxification pathways, specifically the uterus and the liver. The uterus sheds a regular menses as a way of cleansing itself of blood and fluids that are no longer needed when a fertilized egg has not been implanted. When there is hormone disruption it disturbs the flow of this regulated cycle of self-cleansing. To assist with keeping hormones balanced, one of the many roles of the liver is to metabolize and breakdown hormones. When the liver function is disrupted, slowed down, halted, or altered in any way this will cause a continual circulation of hormones such as estrogen, thereby creating an imbalance to hormonal rhythms in an organ system driven by hormones. Therefore, it is not only important for the uterus to be consistently supported but the liver as well. By doing so the liver can maintain a fluidity in its ability to synthesize, metabolize, and detoxify hormones regularly. Considering that toxins are a reoccurring factor in the environment, supporting the role of the detoxification pathways minimizes the impact the toxins can have on not only the reproductive health but your overall health as well.

MEN'S HEALTH

A disrupted endocrine system can directly interfere with male hormone function as well, thereby causing them to be infertile. Viable sperm are necessary for male fertility, and testosterone is the hormone that stimulates the process of reproduction. The process relies heavily on a high level of sperm concentration, the sperm's ability to move rapidly toward its target, and the shape of the sperm, which indicates maturity. All of which are strong indicators of the sperm's ability to quickly race to greet the releasing egg of the lady in waiting. Exposure to the toxic chemicals listed at the beginning of this section as endocrine disruptors have been shown to contribute to male infertility. That list of environmental toxins along with many others (listed in the toxin section) also serve as contributing factors to other health conditions affecting men such as prostate cancer and heart disease.

"The food you eat can be the safest, most powerful form of medicine, or the slowest form of poison."
—Ann Wigmore

PART 2

DAILY TOXIC EXPOSURES

MOST PEOPLE ARE NOT WALKING AROUND CONCERNED ABOUT HOW many toxins they are coming into contact with on a daily basis, and that is a good thing. The amount of toxins that individuals are potentially exposed to can be downright overwhelming. In the upcoming pages of this book I will be highlighting some of the most common toxins, which is still a very extensive list of health hazard contacts that are frequently made knowingly and unknowingly, sometimes controllable and sometimes not. This content, although not complete in its list of all toxins that exist or are encountered regularly, is designed to begin to illuminate more understanding around the topic. Nonetheless, this body of information is not meant to overwhelm you but raise your awareness of the excessiveness of toxins that are being dumped on Americans every day. With raised awareness of the massive amount of toxins that quickly accumulate over time, I want to empower you to choose a healthier option or at the very least intentionally support your built-in detoxification channels so that they don't accumulate into disease. We can accept toxins as a reoccurring part of daily life. You get to choose how you respond to them, but it all begins with being familiar with what they are.

CHAPTER 3

AIR POLLUTANTS

WHAT IS AIR POLLUTION? BREATHING IS REQUIRED TO PROvide the body with necessary oxygen to sustain life. Unfortunately, the air we breathe is not always fresh and clean air but, rather, air that is tainted with pollutants. The Centers for Disease Control and Prevention (CDC) state that air pollution is a leading environmental threat to human health. Air pollution is a physical, biological, or chemical alteration to the air that is considered to be contaminated. This polluted air can contain toxic amounts of dust, fumes, gases, odors, or mixtures of solid particles that are indoors or outdoors. The impact that air pollution has, will not only cause disease, death, or some level of discomfort to humans, it can also be very damaging to other living organisms, crops of food, and the environment in general.

The health impact of toxic air pollutants has been reported at costing more than $100 billion per year in America.[1] It can be concluded that significant improvements of clean air conditions are greatly needed to help reduce or eliminate this toxic burden. Across this country there are power plants, boilers, and cement factories burning coal and other fossil fuels as their energy source; these emissions, filtering into the air, end up compromising the health of the general public. Research has demonstrated a correlation between these air pollutants and decreased wellness among the American population. The adverse effects of exposure to these toxic pollutants being emitted into the air has been shown to impact the health of Americans with increased occurrences of the following: premature births, preterm births, birth defects, low birth weights, cardiovascular diseases (atherosclerosis and heart attacks), chronic respiratory illness (asthma), emergency room visits, and hospital admissions, to name a few. The organic compounds that are emitted from the burning of these toxic energy sources can be particularly damaging to the health of infants and children, whose developing bodies are more vulnerable to cognitive skill disruption that can impact school performance in addition to increased cancer risk.

Unfortunately, out of all the toxic exposures listed in this section, air pollutants are the only toxins that cannot be significantly controlled by an individual. Access to clean air can be variable depending on the community one lives in, which increases or decreases one's air pollution exposure. However, no one regardless of where one lives in the United States is 100 percent safe from the totality of being exposed to toxic air particles. These air pollutants are not only derived from industrial plants, the American population is also exposed to air pollutants through industrial waste fields, automobile emissions, occupational exposures, and cigarette smoke.

LANDFILLS

Solid waste facilities emit foul odors in addition to other air pollution into the environment of nearby residential areas. Research shows that three of the five largest landfills in the United States are in communi-

---

1   Bailey, D. (2011 July) Gasping for Air: Toxic Pollutants Continue to Make Millions Sick and Shorten Lives. {Fact Sheet} Retrieved from http://www.nrdc.org/health/files/airpollutionhealthimpacts.pdf

ties populated predominantly by African Americans or Latinos. Further studies demonstrate that a disproportionate amount of landfills are in areas largely populated by minority groups and secondly, poor income areas. Exposure to landfills can be reduced by residing in residential areas that provide limited to no risk of exposure to toxic nitric oxide and other chemical compounds that produce pollution emitted into the air from the solid waste material.

AUTOMOBILE EMISSIONS

The most up-to-date statistics of 2014 show that the United States has approximately 256 million registered passenger vehicles, coming in second to China, which has the highest amount. These vehicles play the leading role in smog-forming emissions, ozone, and particulate matter circulating in high volumes. In addition, passenger vehicles are also emitting carbon monoxide, nitrogen oxide, and other pollutants into the air that increase a variety of health risks. The World Health Organization reports 3.7 million deaths per year as a result of fine particulate matter found in air pollution. More people are spending longer commute times in their cars, particularly if they live in high-density metropolitan areas. In many of these areas, the distance to work may be short but the time spent in the car has increased because of a larger volume of cars on the road, especially during morning and late afternoon rush hours. With a longer time spent commuting and being on the road during peak times with other cars polluting the air with ozone-, particulate-, and smog-forming emissions, it increases the risk of developing respiratory conditions such as bronchitis and asthma, in addition to other health complications.

OCCUPATIONAL EXPOSURES

Depending on the type of job you have, the industry you work for, or the facility in which you work every day, there can be increased risk of occupational toxic exposures that can eventually lead to occupational disease. Because a full-time schedule is usually a minimum of forty hours per week, that accumulates into almost two thousand hours of exposure per year. Therefore, it is the cumulative effect of being exposed to toxic materials for prolonged hours that can lead to potentially hazardous effects over time; in some cases a more immediate reaction can occur. Those immediate reactions can occur when there is a sensitivity or allergic reaction to allergens or an already compromised immune system, something we see quite often in the sick and elderly communities.

More often than not it is people working manual labor jobs that are more likely to be exposed to these hazardous toxins. In these work environments toxic exposures can include dust particles, chemicals, fibers, fumes, smoke, gases, vapors, mist, and mold. Any of these occupational hazards found in conjunction with a poor ventilation system significantly add to the health risk of those exposed because the toxins are staying stagnate in the air and not circulating out of the environment while clean air is being filtered inside. White collar professionals are not exempt from occupational exposures, as toxic mold and poor ventilation exist in some of the older buildings.

Here are some industries where you could be at an increased risk for occupational toxins that can lead to health problems:

- Aerospace Industry Workers

- Construction Workers

- Cotton, Flax, or Hemp Workers

- Factories

- Farmer or Grain Workers

- Miners

- Flavorings and Popcorn Workers

- Hair and Nail Salons

- Industrial Plants

- Janitorial/Housekeeping/Custodian Workers

- Nylon Fiber Workers

- Professional Drivers (Taxi, Bus, Trucks)

- Sanitation Workers

- Warehouses

- Welders

- Workers exposed to Diesel Fumes

The various elements listed below are hazardous and can cause toxic conditions within the body that lead to respiratory illness and other diseases after repeated exposure (this is not an exhaustive list).

Dust from wood, cotton, coal, asbestos, silica, and talc. Dust from cereal grains, coffee, pesticides, drug or enzyme powders, metals, and fiberglass. Jobs with these types of exposures will include farmers, factory workers, and industrial plant workers.

Fumes from metals that are heated and cooled quickly. This process results in fine, solid particles being carried in the air. Examples of jobs that involve exposure to fumes from metals include welding, smelting, furnace work, pottery making, plastics manufacture, and rubber operations.

Smoke from burning organic materials. Smoke can contain a variety of particles, gases, and vapors, depending on what substance is being burned. Firefighters are at risk of exposure.

Gases such as formaldehyde, ammonia, chlorine, sulfur dioxide, ozone, and nitrogen oxides. Examples of jobs with these exposures include sanitation workers and mortuary workers.

Vapors, which are a form of gas given off by liquids and solvents. Examples of jobs with these exposures include painters, carpet installers, and those working in manufacturing plants that produce solvents.

Mists or sprays from paints, lacquers (such as varnish), hair spray, pesticides, cleaning products, acids, oils, and solvents (such as turpentine). Examples of jobs with these exposures include hair salon workers, painters, farmers, and janitorial or housekeeping workers.

Second- and Third-Hand Cigarette Smoke

Over the past fifteen or so years, many employers, restaurants, bars, and other public places have implemented bans on smoking in their establishments as a public safety concern for people who do not smoke. This limits the risk of exposure and therefore reduces the impact that this secondhand smoke can adversely have on the health of innocent bystanders. Considering this has been a continual conversation in the news, it is clear that the general public has been forewarned about the health dangers of being in the presence of someone who is smoking tobacco-related products. Since that time many smokers no longer smoke in the privacy of their own home when living with non-smokers. Smokers are provided with cigarette breaks on the job so they can go outside to have a few minutes of long, slow drags or quick puffs. Airports have opened special rooms where smokers can go light up before boarding the plane. Safety precautions have been made to protect the rights of smokers' decision to continue smoking if they so choose, but with the proviso that these activities are not putting non-smokers at risk.

What happens when all these provisions are made and the public remains at risk when they interact with smokers? This risk takes place not because someone is smoking in the present moment they are with you; the problem is they have had a cigarette or a pack before coming into your presence. After enjoying their cigarette(s), the nicotine residuals are still on the person—on their hair or their clothes, on the furniture, carpet, and walls, or in their cars.

THIRD-HAND CIGARETTE SMOKE

Nicotine and other chemicals leave their footprint on the smoker and environment; anyone coming into contact with the smoker or the environment in which cigarettes are regularly smoked is still exposed to harmful toxins. Of course, if you happen to get on an elevator for ten stories with someone who has just had a cigarette, it's not a big deal, as you may never see that smoker again. But what happens when that smoker is your spouse, parent, roommate, or someone with whom you carpool to work every day? It is constant exposure overtime that builds up a cumulative effect of these nicotine-filled toxins invading your body and diminishing your health.

In the case of third-hand smoke, research supports that it is newborns, infants, and children whose growing and developing bodies are most at risk to these toxins than any other group.

Although this list of air pollutants is not exhaustive, the information provided here is enough to increase awareness of how you can be impacted by a toxic overload simply from breathing unclean air, whether it is in your neighborhood, place of employment, car, or home. Regardless of how or where your air is being contaminated, the important key to remember is these toxins are significantly altering your health outcomes. Not breathing air for more than four minutes will surely cause irreversible brain damage, and this is not a viable option. Sad to say, unless you choose to work in a different type of profession with better indoor air quality and located in a community known for its great air and your house just happens to be down the street, there is not much else I can recommend to improve this one toxic factor. You may not have control over the air quality outside your home but inside your home you can apply the following tips.

1. Change your air filters on a consistent basis to reduce the amount of circulating dust and allergens in your home.

2. Use a dehumidifier to reduce potential for mold and allergens in your home.

3. Open windows regularly to allow fresh air to circulate and reduce the stagnation of the air quality inside the home.

CHAPTER 4

FOODS

A MERICA HAS BUILT A NATION CENTERED ON CONVENIENCE TO AC-commodate and maintain busy lifestyles and capitalism, even if that means compromising not only the health status of its current population but also jeopardizing the health of future generations. Food is supposed to provide nutrition, and that nutrition plays a variety of roles that include being the primary energy source for the body, regulating the cellular processes of the body, and aiding in cellular growth and tissue repair. There is absolutely a direct correlation between the body's ability to thrive and the types of foods it receives on a regular basis. It is the over-consumption of nutrient-depleted foods and the under-consumption of nutrient rich foods in the body that is the leading causes of heart disease, cancer, and diabetes.

The leading role that food plays in health cannot be substituted with anything else. With advancements in technology, science, along with the permission of the government, has contributed to a substantial manipulation of the foods that stock the grocery store chains. Along the aisles you can purchase a plethora of "food-like" items containing genetically modified organisms (GMOs), additives, and preservatives, just to name a few. Adding GMOs to food make it more convenient for the manufacturer to develop and prolong the shelf life in addition to it being more convenient for the consumer to prepare and/or consume. This has done more to contribute to the decline of health than help it to thrive.

Convenience foods without a doubt save time in the immediate moment, but what is it actually freeing people up to do more of? Right now it

27

is apparent that people are putting in more work hours even when away from the actual work building and less time is being contributed to self-care items like eating a meal while not in a rush. All of these and more are the cumulative impact of what contributes to more illness instead of better health. To cut corners on food preparation now could mean time saved, but that must be paid back later with diminished health, poor quality of life, medications with side effects, surgeries, and frequent doctors' visits.

ADDITIVES AND PRESERVATIVES

The greatest amount of toxins are going to be found in packaged and processed foods. Some of the most common items include baking mixes, breakfast cereals, condiments, cookies, crackers, canned or frozen soups, dairy products, frozen entrees, processed meats, sauces, and snack foods. The amount of toxins are so high because these processed and packaged foods have to be stabilized through chemical processing to ensure safety and appeal upon consumption. Consider the paradox that the same chemicals used to promote consumer safety and appeal are slowly harming and destroying our health over time. Of course, no one wants to eat spoiled luncheon meat, brown canned green beans, sour-smelling ketchup, molded bread, or rancid vegetable oil, but it does come with some consequences.

Chemical-laden food preservatives are added in to maintain the appearance of foods that would normally discolor or turn rancid over time due to oxidization of the product. Preservatives also harness any fungal or bacterial growth and development. Lastly, preservatives will also extend out the shelf life of conventional produce by inhibiting the natural ripening process. The greater the consumption of conventional produce along with packaged and processed foods the greater the toxic exposure.

In addition to preservatives many of the packaged and processed foods have a long list of other additives as well. These direct additives are chemicals used to enhance the flavor, texture, and smell of food products, which after being frozen or sitting on a shelf for months need the additional help to remain appealing and palatable to the public. To keep manufacturing costs low, many of these items are packaged in plastic, aluminum, or paper containers, and the chemicals from these containers can seep into the food product. Therefore, it becomes an indirect food additive and increases our toxic exposure when we consume them.

The leakage of these chemicals into food, water, and other beverages then intensifies in heat, microwave ovens, and direct sunlight. It is important to remember that your first encounter with these products is when they are on the grocery store shelves ready for you to purchase, take home, and consume whenever you are ready as long as it is before the printed expiration date. The journey of these products is much more extensive than that, considering that the product has to be manufactured, packaged, and shipped. And then it will sit for some time in the stockroom before placed on the sales floor. Therefore, you are not aware of what kind of heat these products have been exposed to before they reach you, the consumer.

Currently in the United States there are three thousand food additives listed by the US Food and Drug Administration. When you consider that there are not three thousand different types of foods outside of your basic whole food groups (dairy, eggs, meat, poultry, fish, whole grains, legumes, vegetables, fruits, nuts, and seeds) every item within each category still falls far from one thousand. The list of additives is far more extensive than the list of foods; for the sake of this book, and to simply increase your awareness, I have only listed the most common additives and preservatives, particularly those that have been associated with health risks.

There is a wide range of controversy over the health impacts of the ingredients you will see on the pages to follow, with some sources affirming that a long list of poor health effects can be attributed to these additives and preservatives. Those medical conditions can include cancer of many forms, heart disease, asthma, allergic reactions, ADHD, neurological and cognitive development of fetuses and children, infertility, decreased immune response, and so many more. While other sources contend that there are no measurable ill health effects, many of these chemicals in the said amounts listed below are currently in US food and beverage products. This may indeed be true if people were consuming one serving per day of food and beverage products containing the additives, but what looks small on an isolated consumption scale quickly becomes big when society is driven by faster and more convenient, prepackaged and processed foods as a part of every meal, every day, over the course of one's lifetime.

In addition, it is not just the high consumption of one additive but the synergistic impact of several chemical-filled additives that must be taken into account as well, while also considering their cumulative impact. You could be the parent who packs your child's lunch for school because you think it's a better alternative to what is served in the cafeteria. Your simple lunch may include a whole wheat sandwich with prepackaged turkey, a slice of processed American cheese, mayo, mustard, a piece of romaine lettuce, a tomato slice, a bag of Sun Chips, a juice box, a packaged fruit cocktail cup, and a couple of Oreo cookies.

This one meal alone has at least *seventeen different additives and preservatives,* not including pesticides or potential genetic modifications. This is the nutrition you have now exposed your child to so that he or she can be energized for the next few hours. Keep in mind that this is just one meal on one day of the week, and there are at least twenty other meals and snacks to be accounted for.

It is typical that people are often too tired to cook after work, therefore it becomes easy to make a fast-food stop after work, pop a frozen dinner into the microwave, or warm up a meal from a box or a can where you just add water and/or cooked meat. For many Americans this is a regular part of their daily lives and, more often than not, none of the items are organic—meaning untampered or unaltered without all the chemical-laden ingredients or genetic modifications. With that being said, it does not take long for exposures to the additives and preservatives to quickly add up. As demonstrated, you can see how by the end of a week or month, the toxic exposure that you are potentially receiving from your food can grow exponentially and quickly. For those who are charged with the special responsibility of caring for and raising children, the toxic exposure is of even greater concern because of the fragility of their underdeveloped bodies, which are now being introduced to more substances that arrest their growth and development instead of enhancing it.

COMMON FOOD PRESERVATIVES CAN INCLUDE:

Propionic acid (also seen as calcium propionate), which prevents bread from molding can be found in baked goods and processed meats. Attributed to behavioral problems and sleep disturbances in children.

Sodium nitrite or sodium nitrate used to prevent spoilage and add flavor in cured meats such as bacon, jerky, deli meats, and smoked salmon. Health risks include carcinogens, heart disease, and increase diabetes risk.

Benzoates (also seen as sodium or potassium benzoate) used in acidic foods like salad dressings, pickles, condiments, and carbonated beverages. Known to trigger or exacerbate asthma, allergic rhinitis, and ADHD.

Sulfites prevent discoloration and browning and can be found in numerous products such as processed baked goods, pickles, olives, salad dressing, powdered sugar, lobster, shrimp, scallops, canned clams, fruit fillings, and potatoes. In addition to beverages that include fruit juices, beer, and cocktail mixes. May exacerbate allergic rhinitis and asthma.

Butylated hydroxyanisole (BHA) helps keep foods from going rancid. Found in high-fat products such as meats, butter, baked goods, snack foods, and dehydrated potatoes, chewing gum, and beer. Possible human carcinogen.

Butylated hydroxytoluene (BHT) keeps foods from developing an odor while also preserving the color and flavor. BHT can be found in foods that contain high amounts of fats and oils, shortenings, and cereals. It can also be found in other products such as jet fuels, rubber petroleum products, transformer oil, and embalming fluid. Possible human carcinogen.

Potassium Sorbate stops the growth and spread of harmful bacteria and mold. Found in syrups, cheese, yogurt, dip, pickles, jams, baked goods, wine, soft drinks, in addition to dehydrated meats and fruits. Can cause allergic reactions.

COMMON FOOD ADDITIVES CAN INCLUDE:

Carrageenan acts as a thickener or emulsifier and creates a smooth texture to foods. Can be found in foods such as ice cream, yogurt, cottage cheese, and non-dairy milks (almond and coconut). Causes inflammation.

Propylene Glycol acts as a thickener and texturizer in foods. Edible items containing this chemical can include flavored ice tea, packaged frosting, boxed cake mixes, prepackaged baked goods, ice cream, and salad dressings. It can also be found in many personal hygiene products, laundry detergents, and used as antifreeze for cars and airplanes. High levels can cause skin irritation along with neurotoxic and cardiovascular issues.

Aspartame is an artificial sweetener found in many beverages, beverage mixes, yogurts, mints, chewing gum, tabletop sweeteners, and many other baked goods and mixes labeled as "sugar free." Increased risk of cancer, migraines, and other health ailments.

Cochineal (red coloring), which is derived from a South American insect, can also be found in makeup. May initiate or provoke allergic reactions in some individuals. The WHO requires that ingredient be listed to warn consumers in case a severe allergic reaction occurs.

Titanium Dioxide (white coloring) is found in candies, sweets, and chewing gum. Also can be found in toothpaste and sunscreens. Can cause oxidative stress, inflammation, immune response, and may be a possible carcinogen.

Monosodium Glutamate (MSG) is a flavor enhancer found associated commonly with Chinese restaurant foods, but can also be found in chips, canned soups, snack foods, frozen meals, and salad dressings. Can have harmful effects on people with diabetes and/or hypertension.

Trans Fats/ aka Partially Hydrogenated Oils are found in vegetable shortening, margarine, crackers, packaged frosting, pie crust, canned biscuits, non-dairy creamer, microwave popcorn, and packaged cookies and cakes. Raises low-density lipoprotein (LDL) cholesterol, carcinogens, increases cardiovascular disease risk.

High-Fructose Corn Syrup (HFCS) is found in baked goods, canned fruits, dairy products, breakfast cereals, condiments, candy, candy bars, sodas and other carbonated beverages, and fruit drinks. Health risk include premature aging, diabetes, increased plaque in arteries, and immune system damage.

Agricultural Chemicals (Pesticides). There are a wide range of chemical compounds that include herbicides, fungicides, insecticides, rodenticides, and others that are designed to protect the quality of the crops. Linked to health effects that include immune suppression, endocrine disruption, cancer, diminished intelligence, and reproductive abnormalities.

Genetically Modified Organisms (GMOs) are defined by the WHO as organisms (i.e., plants, animals, or microorganisms) in which the genetic material (DNA) has been altered in a way that does not occur naturally by mating and/or natural re-combination. The technology is often called "modern biotech-nology" or "gene technology," sometimes also "recombinant DNA technology" or "genetic engineering." It allows selected individual genes to be transferred from one organism into another, and also between nonrelated species. "Unexpected effects" and health risks posed by genetic engineering can include toxicity, allergic reactions, antibiotic resistance, im-mune system-suppression, cancer, and loss of nutrition.

Hormones. Steroid hormone drugs that include both synthetic and natural estrogen, testosterone, and progesterone to in-crease the growth rate of livestock that then increases the amount of food production. Another synthetic hormone called recombinant bovine somatotropin (rBST) is a growth hor-mone given to cows to increase their milk production. With unnatural increases in milk production the cows develop mas-titis, which is inflammation of the mammary glands that get treated with antibiotics (read below for more information on this additive). When consumers intake these hormone-filled foods they are being exposed to additional hormones that are above and beyond the body's own cycle of natural hormone function. Please see the section on endocrine disruption for more information on how exogenous hormones (those made outside the body) impact health.

Antibiotics. The meat industry feeds these drugs to poultry, cattle, and pigs regularly to help them increase in weight more quickly and also to treat infections and diseases that can be a by-product of their confined living conditions. Health risk include gut dysbiosis (imbalance between your good and bad gut bacteria), which can lead to yeast overgrowth and a vari-ety of other digestive disturbances. Repetitive antibiotic expo-sure can make humans more susceptible to infections that are resistant to antibiotics.

Just like air, food is also a very vital element to sustainable life. As demonstrated earlier there is an interconnectedness between the toxic exposures that foods have prior to arriving on our meal plate and the good or bad impact those foods have on our health. Depending on the quality of the food we consume they can either be providing necessary nutrients to our bodies or high levels of toxicity that can eventually cause us harm. Unlike air, we have the power to control many aspects of the quality and types of food we eat. And if we are very ambitious we can even control how it is grown by doing it ourselves, if we so desire.

Below is a list of the top eight things you can do to reduce your dietary toxic exposure and improve your health.

1. When shopping at conventional grocery store chains, shop mostly on the periphery of the store. It is this outer perimeter that has all of your whole foods and those that have been minimally processed such as produce, fresh breads, nuts and seeds, dairy, and meats. Avoid shopping for items down the aisles of the grocery store as much as possible since they are usually heavily processed and packaged, with the exception of whole grains and legumes.

2. Read food labels. If you are not in the habit of doing so already, begin to read the labels to your foods and only purchase those products with ingredients you can pronounce. You don't have to wait until the FDA does a new research study to make a decision regarding chemical-filled ingredients not being the most optimal choice for you and your family. If a chemical is strong enough to de-ice an airplane (propylene glycol), do you really want to consume it in your peach-flavored iced tea or your salad dressing? Of course not. There are healthier options available that will give you great tasting nutritious foods without the health consequences of the various additives and preservatives.

3. Buy organic produce as much as possible that are free of GMOs and pesticides. Some conventional produce is more heavily sprayed with pesticides than others, so the healthiest choice is always chemical-free produce. When your choices are limited by finances or what is available at your local grocer refer to the heavily toxic conventional produce versus the conventional produce list that has fewer pesticides found below.

High Pesticide Contamination (Avoid Conventional, Buy Organic only):

• Apples

• Celery

- Cherry Tomatoes
- Collard Greens
- Cucumbers
- Grapes
- Hot Peppers
- Kale
- Nectarines
- Peaches
- Snap Peas
- Spinach
- Strawberries
- Sweet Bell Peppers
- White Potatoes

LESS PESTICIDE CONTAMINATION (BUY ORGANIC OR CONVENTIONAL)

- Asparagus
- Avocado
- Cabbage
- Cantaloupe
- Cauliflower
- Eggplant
- Grapefruit
- Kiwi

- Mangoes

- Onions

- Papayas

- Pineapples

- Sweet Corn

- Sweet Peas

- Sweet Potatoes

4. When you do make selections of pre-packaged or processed food items, such as soup, cereals, condiments, whole grains, nuts, seeds, etc., choose an organic version to avoid additional toxic chemical exposure. Purchase pre-made foods from hot bars from healthy establishments that list their ingredients.

5. Cook your own whole foods meals at home. Yes, that means going back to the basics and making meals from scratch just like grandma used to make. When you prepare your own meals from scratch you get to control each and every ingredient that goes into the meal. You can also choose natural herbs and spices that not only make your "real" food taste flavorful such as garlic, onions, and cilantro, they also have a variety of health benefits that protect you from disease.

6. Make plant-based meals your dietary staple, while limiting or eliminating daily or weekly meat and dairy consumption.

7. When consuming meat and dairy products, eat meats that have been grass-fed, organic poultry, and wild-caught fish. Ensure that both meat and dairy products are free of any hormones, antibiotics, or other additives and preservatives. Choose leaner cuts of meat and dairy products that are low in saturated fats.

8. Eat at least five to nine servings of vegetables and fruits per day with at least three to four of those servings being raw: a salad, a smoothie, or cut-up veggies and whole fruit.

CHAPTER 5

DRINKING WATER

H UMAN BEINGS ARE ONLY ONE OF ALL LIVING ORGANISMS WHOSE
survival depends on consuming adequate hydration. It is safe to
say that water is the key to life for all living things, but as our
bodies are comprised of more than 60 percent water, it is responsible for
the regulation of many cellular processes. The fluidity of water and its
capacity to flow from place to place helps to supply nutrients to cells in
addition to carrying waste products out of the body via the kidneys. Water also plays many roles in the digestive track by softening, diluting, and
liquefying our food to enhance its digestion. An adequate daily intake of
water is important in ensuring that these processes are sustained and
supported throughout the day, every day. Because of the vital role that
water plays, not only is the quantity of consumption important but the
quality of water is equally as important to support the bodily functions.

Unfortunately, our American tap water supply has become so toxic
that many people opt to purchase bottled water and in-home water filtration systems than subject themselves to further toxic exposure. Currently
the tap water supply, which comes largely from the rivers and lakes, is
regulated by the US Environmental Protection Agency (EPA). Before tap
water reaches its consumers it is commonly treated through a process of
coagulation, filtration, and disinfection to prepare it for safe consumption. By the time the water runs through our particular tap it is supposed
to be safe from the various toxic contaminants that can be harmful in
large quantities; however, some toxins survive past the treatment process. These toxins can include disinfectant by-products; heavy metals,

such as mercury and lead; and medications.

In addition to chemicals found in water, new studies have revealed trace amounts of prescriptions and over-the-counter drugs that have entered the water system via urinary excretion of patients consuming medications as well as those discarding whole pills in the toilet. More than half of the waste water plants that were tested around the country had medications that included oxycodone; hypertensive medications, Tylenol, and Ibupropren. Among these drugs, high blood pressure medication was ranked highest among the pharmaceuticals found in water.

Technology has improved to the point of being capable of tracing small amounts of medications and there has been an increase in the use of prescribed drugs (reported as 70 percent of people are on at least one medication). The long-term impact of this exposure on human health is currently unknown. Precautionary measures have not been developed on ways to safely remove these chemicals from the water supply without causing additional public risks.

It is important to note that medications in the water supply have adversely affected the aquatic life, particularly with male fish developing eggs when exposed to estrogen. As mentioned in the earlier chapter what impacts the health of our food and beverage supply will also impact the health of those of us consuming it. Making a conscious choice about the source of water we consume is a controllable factor in our toxic exposure. It is not necessary to wait until further studies prove or disprove the negative health impacts of toxins in our public water supply. It is apparent that we live with a flawed system that may sometimes place the importance of budgetary cuts over the health of its citizens. The 2015 water crisis in Flint, Michigan, is just the latest example of a municipality that changed its water source and reduced funding for water treatment, allowing lead and iron to proliferate in its supply.

There are no safe levels for lead in the body, especially for children and developing fetuses whose exposure can cause irreversible neurological consequences. Therefore, this type of public neglect should never be acceptable, regardless of the economic status of the community impacted. Of course, the lead in the water supply in Flint is not an occurrence we hear about often, but it is an example of what can happen when we depend heavily on a financially driven government to reduce our toxic exposures when it competes with their budget goals. Whenever possible, as frequently as possible, choose self-empowerment to reduce your own controllable toxic risk factors. This is the key to creating a personal environment in which you are not just merely surviving but thriving. Considering water is the key to life, drink it clean, fresh, and chemical free as often as possible.

Recommended tips for preferred water consumption include:
1.   For daily water intake and washing produce choose purified water sources that include filtered or spring water.

2.   Reserve alkaline water for short-term periods of fourteen days or less for detoxification purposes only to avoid significantly disrupting the body's natural pH levels.

3.   Drink at least half your body weight in ounces of water per day. An example would be if you weighed one hundred and fifty pounds, you should drink 75 ounces of water per day, or 9.5 cups.

4.   Carry a large glass or stainless steel bottle with you through-out the day to keep track of water consumption and to ensure that you always have the best source of water already on your person.

5.   Use a purified water filtration system at home and refill per-sonal containers as necessary to reduce the need for purchas-ing bottled water while out. You can also refill larger three- and five-gallon water jugs at local health food stores and other grocery chains for home use if you do not have an in-house filtration system.

6.   Avoid consuming plastic bottle water (read more about this in chapter 9 on household products).

CHAPTER 6

CHEMICAL SUBSTANCES

RECREATIONAL DRUGS, CIGARETTES, AND ALCOHOL

Sometimes those fun, stress-relieving, wind-down opportunistic experiences some partake in after a long hard day at work or school, on the weekends while hanging out with friends, or those vacation times of the year can expose the body to unnecessary toxic substances. Having a cigarette to calm your nerves, that business meeting over drinks, inhaling a couple of lines to take the edge off and jump-start your night of partying, or even that doctor-prescribed painkiller you received from someone else can all feel very therapeutic during the time of consumption. Yes, it feels great in the moment to have your burdens lifted as your neurological function becomes altered to release pleasurable dopamine, uninhibit your actions, or momentarily eliminate your pain sensation.

As you party like a rock star, your body is being exposed to a significant amount of toxins that can damage your nerve cells and overtax the liver. However good recreational drugs, alcohol, and cigarettes may make you feel in that moment, the cellular damage to the body, especially after repeated use, is not worth the benefits of your temporary "fix" of choice. Although alcohol is more socially acceptable "in public" and can be used more safely in moderation than recreational drugs, it is still toxic to the liver where it is metabolized.

This specific section of toxins unlike any of the others mentioned in this book, are 100 percent individually selective—unlike air, food, water, pesticides, personal care products, and such, these substances are not needed for anything. Any given person can live a full, productive life without ever encountering any of these substances and the toxicity they produce. Therefore, the only recommendation that can be made for this category is as cliché as they come, but still rings true: "JUST SAY NO!"

PRESCRIPTION AND OVER-THE-COUNTER MEDS

Prescription and over-the-counter medications are providing you with the relief to your symptom, but searching for the root cause of the problem and correcting it from that level puts the body back in balance to self-repair as needed (if it has not been irreversibly damaged). Many people seek out over-the-counter drugs to provide immediate yet temporary relief from whatever health ailment they are facing. When your body feels discomfort it is not crying out that it is lacking ibuprofen, aspirin, or other pain killers; it is notifying you that there is a disturbance somewhere and once you correct that disturbance the symptom will no longer be there.

However, the average person is conditioned to handle medical situations with a doctor-prescribed or self-purchased medication that quiets the symptom but fails to address the true nature of the problem. Let's say the engine oil light comes on in your car. Just because you disconnect the light switch for the engine oil light does not change the fact that the car is still in need of oil. Neglecting to change the oil will produce a problem with your engine over time because your vehicle is not receiving the lubrication it needs to operate. If the engine oil light is blinding or distracting you while you drive, it is very important that you do something to turn it off so you can continue to drive with ease until you can change the oil, but the oil *itself* must be changed to prevent a greater mechanical problem.

It is the same with our bodies; you should not walk around in pain or discomfort but, while quieting the immediate symptoms, the root cause should also be evaluated and addressed so that the correction to the problem is long-lasting instead of temporary.

I am in no way saying that if you have been prescribed prescription medications to stop taking them; what I am saying is that even those unnatural chemical substances with legitimate therapeutic value carry the consequences of increasing your toxic exposure. As beneficial as the pain-relieving, bacteria-killing, blood-pressure-decreasing, insulin-producing, cancer-destroying properties of drugs can be, they are all still unnatural substances made from chemicals, and *chemicals are toxic to the body.*

41

If your physician has prescribed you medications to address your disease process, it is very important that you are intentional about detoxifying on a regular basis so that the body can be supported in keeping your risk of toxic overload low. Taking medications in addition to the variety of other toxic exposures mentioned in this book creates a cumulative impact that can only be addressed by intentionally detoxifying the body and supporting its cleansing pathways on a regular basis. More details about how to do this can be found in Chapter 13, "Navigating a Successful Detox."

CHAPTER 7

PERSONAL CARE PRODUCTS

P RODUCTS THAT ARE MAKING US BEAUTIFUL ON THE OUTSIDE COULD slowly be killing us on the inside. Some ingredients found in common name-brand personal care products have been found to be industrial chemical agents, carcinogenic, allergenic, neurotoxic, and endocrine disruptors.

The skin, which you will learn more about in the next section of this book, is the human body's largest organ and is highly absorptive. Certain medications and hormones can be applied to the skin for their systemic medicinal effects, meaning they are impacting more far-reaching places in the body other than locally where the topical application is applied. If certain medications seep through the barrier of the skin and into our bloodstream, what about the plethora of products we use every day that are intentionally designed to penetrate the skin as it cleanses, softens, and moisturizes it? Currently there is an abundance of products available on the market (most of which the safety has not been guaranteed by the FDA) that are designed to make us feel fresh and clean and well deodorized. Staying current with your personal hygiene is an absolute must, especially if you are in the company of others; however, what is the true cost of looking and smelling fresh and fabulous?

I have to continue to emphasize that the danger does not lie in one application or even one container that is applied, it is the cumulative load that can lead to toxicity that compromises neurological function, endocrine function, hormone dysregulation, immune function, along with male and female reproductive function. Below is a list of commonly used personal care products and potentially toxic ingredients in them that can be harmful to the body with repeated exposure. This list of products or toxic chemicals inside of them is not meant to be exhaustive but simply to provide enough information to raise your awareness on daily exposure to toxic substances and your ability to choose another option that is less toxic. For a more detailed understanding of these chemicals and the products that contain them, a balanced perspective can be provided between www.fda.org and www.epa.org/skindeep.

The most common toxins found in personal care products are:

Parabens (methyl paraben, ethyl paraben, propyl paraben, isobutyl paraben)—Studied for being an endocrine system disruptor; they can mimic estrogen and bind to estrogen receptors.

Found in: deodorant; antiperspirants; shampoos and conditioners; after shave; shaving cream; makeup; cosmetics; sunscreens; suntan lotion; pharmaceutical drugs; and they are often added to food.

Triclosan—Some animal studies have shown that it alters hormone regulation and can contribute to making bacteria resistant to antibiotics.

Found in: deodorant; antibacterial soaps; body wash; toothpaste; cosmetics, kitchenware; toys; clothing; and furniture.

Propylene Glycol—Can contribute to skin, kidney, and liver damage; it can also cause allergic reactions in people with pre-existing skin allergies.

Found in: a very wide range of products that include shampoos; cosmetics moisturizers; fragrance oils; and foods.

Phthalates (diethylhelxy phthalate, dibutyl phthalate, dimethyl phthalate, diethyl phthalate)—A reasonably anticipated human carcinogen; and endocrine disruptor.

Found in: perfume, hair spray, soap, shampoo, nail polish, nail hardener, and skin moisturizers. They are also used in consumer products such as flexible plastic and vinyl toys, shower curtains, wallpaper, vinyl mini-blinds, food packaging, and plastic wrap.

Methylisothiazolinone—Some studies indicate it as allergenic.

Found in: shampoo, conditioner, body wash, hair color, shower gel, liquid soap, facial wash, and other personal care products.

Toluene—a respiratory irritant.

Found in: personal care products that include fingernail polish, nail hardener, and synthetic fragrances.

Sodium Lauryl Sulfate (SLS); **Sodium Laureth Sulfate** (SLES); **Ammonium Lauryl Sulfate** (ALS)—skin irritant; contaminated with dioxane, a studied carcinogen.

Found in: makeup, hair color, scalp treatments, shampoo, toothpaste, body washes, bath oils/salts, liquid hand soap, and laundry detergent.

Formaldehyde—carcinogen and skin irritant

Found in: hair straightening products, body wash, liquid hand soaps, and nail hardener.

When purchasing common personal hygiene products it is important to read ingredient labels. To minimize your toxin exposure, refer to the list below to avoid products that have the associated chemicals listed as ingredients. For a list of safe products among specified name brands refer to the www.epa.org/skindeep for more detailed information.

Product Type	Toxic Ingredient(s)
Deodorant	Parabens
	Trisclosan
Antiperspirants	Parabens
Shampoo & Conditioners	Parabens
	Phthalates
	Methylisothiazolinone
Lotions & Skin moisturizers	Phthalates
Sunscreen	Parabens
Makeup	Parabens
	Phthalates
	SLS
	Propylene Glycol
Nail Polish & Remover	Phthalates
	Toluene
	Propylene Glycol

Nail Hardener   Formaldehyde

                                           Toluene

                                           Phthalates

Acne Products   Triclosan

Baby Products   Phthalates

Creams; lotions; oils; wipes

Infant soap; shampoo & body wash

Hair Color   SLS

                                           SLES

                                           ALS

Hair Spray   Phthalates

Scalp Treatments   SLS

Chemical Straighteners   Formaldehyde

Synthetic Fragrances   Toluene

                                           Propylene Glycol

Toothpaste	Triclosan
	SLS
Liquid Hand Soap	SLS
	Formaldehyde
Aftershave	Parabens
Shaving Cream	Triclosan

There is something about stepping out of a soothing hot bath or a shower, whether it is routine cleansing or a therapeutic way in which you wind down. Either way it makes you feel good and clean. Getting cleaned up and making yourself presentable to yourself and the rest of the world can be accomplished in ways that will not eventually make you sick because of repetitive long-term applications. Trying a preventive measure for the next twenty years will serve you better than putting toxins on your face, hair, teeth, nails, and skin every day for the rest of your life.

Years ago, after my grandmother was diagnosed with breast cancer, her oncologist told her to begin using a natural deodorant as a supportive measure to the radiation she was receiving. I discovered this during my time visiting with her and noticed she had the same natural deodorant I had been using for about five years prior. The difference being that I was using it for disease prevention so that my armpits can have the freedom to detoxify my body by removing impurities via sweat whenever they needed to without me blocking the process, which is opposite of what antiperspirants do. However, my grandmother was using it as part of her cancer treatment to ensure that there would not be a lymphatic buildup due to blocked sweat glands from her antiperspirant. I only wished that one of her doctors would have given her these same recommendations decades earlier before she had to succumb to daily radiation treatments, and frequent doctors' visits. Using an antiperspirant is one of many examples of products you apply to your body daily or several times a day that is safe for a few applications, but what about daily applications for decades? If all you used was one product for personal hygiene, it might not be as bad but when you combine it with all the products you apply to smell good and look good, the toxic exposure increases exponentially and quickly.

Tips for reducing toxic load of personal care products

1. Visit the personal care and beauty products aisle at your local health food store or natural beauty boutiques instead of your multipurpose supermarkets or conventional beauty supply stores for hygiene and makeup supplies that are natural and free from harmful chemicals.

2. Read product label to ensure it is free from toxins listed above.

3. When in doubt, if you can't eat it, think twice about applying it to your skin. For moisturizing options consider natural oils such as (olive, coconut, almond, avocado, and shea butter).

4. Take your own natural beauty products to your next manicure/pedicure or hair and make-up appointment, or choose an establishment that uses a natural product line sufficient for you. Just because you choose the natural way does not mean you have to look and feel any less fabulous on the inside or out.

5. Save antiperspirant applications for special occasions like public speaking or first dates when you want to look cool even though you are a nervous wreck on the inside. For all other times, find a natural deodorant that works; this can be a bit challenging at first to find one that holds all day but the less toxic your body becomes the easier it will be to find the right natural application for your body.

CHAPTER 8

HOUSEHOLD PRODUCTS

EVERY DAY IN OUR HOME ENVIRONMENT WE DO A VARIETY OF TASKS that are necessary to keep our humble abode running smoothly. It is important to us that, just like our bodies, our living spaces are kept clean and smelling fresh as often as possible. We do not want streaks across our windows and mirrors, insects crawling on our walls, or that caked-up spillage in our ovens that fills the house with a burnt odor every time we bake something new. After spending time preparing meals, who wants to waste time letting pots and pans soak when everyone knows nonstick cookware is so much easier to clean? Who can forget about all the leftovers that must be put away in the plastic storage containers we clean out and reuse over and over again because they are lightweight, convenient, easily accessible, easily disposable, and cheap to purchase. These are just some of the many toxins that are unknowingly lurking around our homes every day.

Many of our most common go-to household products that we use to clean our toilet bowls, scrub our bathtubs, mop our floors, disinfect the countertops, deodorize the air, polish our furniture, and get the baked-on crust out of our ovens are filled with toxic chemicals that impact our health. As important as it is to keep a clean environment, for many households, use of certain products presents a significant health risk, especially for those with pre-existing medical conditions such as asthma and allergies. Conventional household products may be purchased for the low sales price of two for five dollars, but the ultimate impact on health can become very costly. Associated US healthcare costs for asthma alone, which can be caused or triggered by toxic chemicals found in cleaning products, have been reported to be more than $37 billion annually.

There are a wide range of products on the market that utilize ingredients that act as endocrine disruptors, carcinogens, and allergens. These products are also known to be neurotoxic and can contribute to respiratory distress and other health hazards. Unfortunately for consumers, cleaning product manufacturers are not required to list ingredients on their products so that buyers can be aware of what they are exposing themselves to. To review a more detailed list of specific name-brand household products that have been identified as very toxic to consumers, please visit www.ewg.org/cleaners/hallofshame. Below is a list of common toxins, their health impacts, and the types of products they can be found in. Considering that it is possible that you may not see these or any other ingredients listed on the products you purchase, utilize this list to help you make an informed decision regarding continual use of conventional household products or switching over to something more natural and safer for you, your family, and the environment.

Common toxins found in household products are:

Quaternary Ammonium Compounds—found in antibacterial household cleaners, fabric softener sheets, and liquids.

Health risks: skin irritant; can potentially alter hormone regulation and contribute to bacteria-resistant antibiotics.

Phthalates—found in household products that have a fragrance such as dish-washing soap and air freshener.

Health Risks: an endocrine disruptor and a reasonably anticipated human carcinogen.

Sodium Hydroxide—found in oven cleaners & drain openers

Health Risks: a strong corrosive and powerful irritant by all routes of exposure (inhalation, ingestion, skin contact, and eye contact). It can cause severe burns and permanent damage to any tissue it contacts.

Perchloroethylene OR "PERC"—found in dry cleaning

solutions, upholstery and carpet cleaners, and spot removers

Health Risks: neurotoxic and skin irritant.

Sodium Hypochlorite (Bleach)—found in an abundance of household products that include but not limited to laundry whitening products, toilet bowl cleaners, scouring powders, and mildew removers.

Health Risks: can cause asthma or aggravate pre-existing asthmatic conditions.

Triclosan—found in antibacterial hand soaps and liquid dish-washing detergent

Health Risks: some animal studies have shown that it alters hormone regulation and can contribute to making bacteria resistant to antibiotics.

Ammonia—found in glass cleaner and jewelry cleaner

Health Risks: respiratory, skin, and eye irritant.

Household cleaning products are purposefully designed to destroy, kill, and disinfect odors, bacteria, and any other organisms that creep into your home. If you are not a fan of inhaling and coming into contact with a variety of toxic exposures around your home that can impact the health of you and your family, you have options. Below are a few tips to reduce your exposure to toxic household cleaning supplies.

1. While cleaning your home, wear gloves and a face mask to limit contact of exposure to toxic chemicals.

2. Open the windows of your home while cleaning to circulate fresh air and reduce respiratory impact of chemicals being used.

3. Purchasing safer products made with less toxic and more natural ingredients can significantly decrease your risk of household toxins. Visiting the cleaning aisle at your local health food stores will provide you with a variety of household cleaning products that are made with safer ingredients.

4. Make many of your own cleaning solutions with natural ingredients found around the house such as baking soda (a nonabrasive scrub) and white vinegar (a natural disinfectant). Essential oils such as tea tree and eucalyptus can be added for their antimicrobial effects, as well as lavender or citrus oils for added aromatic pleasure. Instead of spending money on a variety of toxic cleaning products, invest in a spray bottle, a gallon of vinegar, and a large box of baking soda. This will serve as a multipurpose household cleaner that is not only cheap but safe too. Here are just a few products you can make yourself with these three simple ingredients mixed with water as a natural cleaning alternative.

HEALTHIER ALTERNATIVES FOR COMMON PRODUCTS

Be aware that when mixing baking soda and vinegar together it causes a chemical reaction of fizzing, so make sure that your mixing container is large enough to contain the fizz without spillage.

MULTIPURPOSE HOUSEHOLD CLEANER

Use a spray bottle mixed with 1/2 cup of white vinegar, 2 tbsp. of baking soda, 10-15 drops of and essential oil (any citrus, tea tree, or eucalyptus), fill remainder of spray bottle with water. Shake well before applying.

OVEN CLEANER

Mixing baking soda with just enough water to make a paste, apply paste to a warm oven by spreading with a plastic spatula throughout oven with extra attention on caked on grime. Allow applied mixture to sit overnight and use a white vinegar and water mixture to spray and wipe down the following day.

AIR FRESHENER

Mix 1 tbsp. of baking soda with 5-10 drops of your favorite essential oil into a small dish. Fill a spray bottle with distilled water and pour baking soda mixture into the bottle. For a stronger scent add more essential oil drops. Shake well before applying. Mist can be sprayed in the air, on furniture, or carpet to deodorize the room.

*You can also use an essential oil burner or diffuser with your

choice of natural essential oils as another natural fragrance alternative.

FABRIC SOFTENER

Pre-mix 1 cup of baking soda, 15–20 drops of your favorite essential oil (lavender) and 1 cup of water. Obtain a 1 gallon container and pour in pre-mix, add 6 cups of white vinegar, and 6 cups of water. Shake together contents. Add ½ cup to rinse cycle of each load of laundry, for smaller loads reduce to ¼ cup.

INSECTICIDES

Healthier Alternative—because pesticides are designed to kill various living organisms and control disease there is likely going to be some toxicity involved. But you can reduce your exposure amount and severity with a less toxic product. Safer versions of these products are available for purchase by searching for certified green products when choosing the best pesticides for your home. In addition to tips to reduce risk listed on the previous page, for insecticides it is important to keep a clean environment free of spills and crumbs on the countertops and floors, as well as to cover all food to limit insect attraction.

Other than cleaning products that we use on a regular basis in our homes, there are other frequent toxic exposures lurking around in our cabinets, cupboards, stove tops, and refrigerators. Those additional daily used products would include our cookware, utensils, and storage containers. They may seem like innocent bystanders, but they really are not because of the toxins that are being released into our food and beverage supply as a result of using them.

OTHER TOXIC PRODUCTS

Nonstick cookware and kitchen utensils—the coating that makes Teflon pans nonstick is polytetrafluoroethylene, or PTFE for short, and has been linked to cancer and birth defects.

Healthier Alternative—using pots, pans, and baking dishes made of cast iron, stainless steel, and unglazed glass are better options for cooking. In addition to using stainless steel or wooden or bamboo utensils for meal preparations along with silverware for eating.

Plastics are almost as ubiquitous as toxins are. In 2014 the global production of plastic for that year exceeded 300 million metric tons—a tremendous amount of plastic. Our daily exposure to plastics is everywhere integrated into every part of human life. It can be found in largest circulation as containers, with many of those contained or covered items being something that people place either in their mouths or on their skin such as food and personal care products. Depending on the product most manufacturers use plastic whenever possible for food packaging while local grocers use plastic wrap to seal in freshness of meats and in-house baked goods. Every day many Americans are storing leftovers into plastic storage containers, using plastic wrap as a lid to cover a dish; placing sandwiches and other foods into resealable plastic bags, eating with plastic utensils during lunch at school or work, and who can forget the overflow of plastic water and beverage bottles that are everywhere we go.

Since few people are drinking from their home faucets these days, it is not unusual to go to someone's house and be offered a bottled water instead of a glass of water, which was more commonplace twenty years ago. Because these plastics are in direct contact with food and beverages, its chemicals are leeching into our dietary products, quickly accumulating over shorter periods of time. This accumulation of toxins intensifies through the use of other products that make contact with the human bloodstream, which are also contained by plastics.

Plastic is the typical container that holds personal hygiene products and cosmetics, the items you apply to your skin on a frequent basis. You can already imagine how often throughout a given day or week you consume food packaged in a plastic container, liquid hand soap, skin moisturizer, toothpaste, deodorant, or shampoo without a second thought. As mentioned in the previous sections, not only are you subjected to the toxic chemicals that are inside of foods, beverages, and personal care products but the problem becomes two-fold when the consumable product and the product container are both toxic exposures. This is just an example of one basic day in the life of an average American; unfortunately, for most of us, this accumulation of plastic toxic exposures dates back to infancy and toddlerhood when every toy had to be first explored by the mouth. As you can see, the lifetime of exposure to plastics is long and deep, which makes regular detoxification even more imperative to reduce the ramifications of the seemingly inescapable health burden wrapped in convenience.

There is no argument that plastic is absolutely an incredible resource to have around the house, car, workplace, sporting event, extracurricular activity, or wherever we may be engaging with life. Plastic is cheap, lightweight, malleable, disposable, water-proof, and easy to wipe down, all of which can be a godsend for anyone who has small children. These characteristics along with many more make it the ideal choice for many manufacturers and consumers alike to choose plastic as a handy multipurpose product. While useful in so many industries, its cumulative impact remains as a threat to human health. The quick accumulation from such an extensive range of plastic exposures can lead to many harmful health effects, particularly those deriving from endocrine disruption.

Exposure to the chemicals found in plastics include:

Bisphenol-A (BPA), which is used in a wide variety of plastic products including the inside lining of food cans. BPA is an extensive animal-studied chemical that has demonstrated in-utero dangers for fetuses that lead to abnormal breast, prostate, and brain development. Studies have also indicated reproductive disorders that include infertility, early female puberty, and feminizing of male organs in fetuses. BPA acts as a synthetic hormone by mimicking estrogen.

Phthalates—another chemical found in many plastics (discussed in previous sections), which once again serves as an endocrine disruptor by interfering with the production, signaling, and interaction of hormones within the body.

Dioxin—serves as a human carcinogen and an endocrine disruptor.

Styrene—the plastic found in Styrofoam has been classified as a possible human carcinogen.

On any given day the average person is exposed to numerous plastic products and, at this point in the book, phthalates have been mentioned as a toxin in numerous product exposures. It's safe to say that the cumulative toxic exposure to this one chemical is high. When you combine this toxic exposure with the other toxins mentioned it is not only a cumulative health hazard but also a synergistic one. The synergy (toxins working together as a combined unified force) has not been studied to determine long-term health impacts, although current research indicates that the estimated health care costs associated with chemicals in plastics is at least $28 billion per year.

For the general public, it would be a lot safer to begin reducing the exposure to these various chemical as much as possible to reduce potential life-altering effects that have not yet been studied.

SIX WAYS TO REDUCE PLASTICS EXPOSURE

1. Purchase a reusable glass or stainless steel water bottle to carry with you throughout the day to avoid plastic water bottle consumption.

2. Store leftovers, lunches, snacks, and other foods in glass or stainless steel containers.

3. Avoid using or storing plastic or Styrofoam that contains food or beverages in high heat places such as microwave ovens, direct sunlight in cars or homes to minimize additional leaching. Microwave foods in CorningWare, glass containers, or unbleached paper plates.

4. Look for "BPA-Free" stickers when purchasing toys and other plastic containers as a safer option.

5. Store your natural liquid soap and other frequently used products in glass pump jars and containers.

6. Invest in some (non-plastic) reusable traveling utensils to use at school, work, or other meals away from home.

CHAPTER 9

RELATIONSHIPS

AS PART OF MY HOLISTIC APPROACH TO CLEANSING, IT IS IMPORTANT to note that another primary toxic exposure in our daily lives can also be our relationships, which also happens to be a controllable toxic exposure.

Toxic relationships can show up in our lives in our most significant relationships that usually occur with spouses, romantic partners, parents, and friends. These are all the most valued relationships people proclaim to love and care very deeply about and they also have a considerable level of influence over our daily lives. Because there is love and caring involved, which should be mutual, it is also reasonable to expect that there is mutual control, respect, compassion, consideration, and support. Relationships are necessary to help nurture the growth and development of each of us into a greater version of ourselves, which means that they should be truthful yet uplifting, character building not destructive, and energy giving instead of depleting. There is no room for jealousy, envy, deceit, manipulation, domination, or controlling behavior in a healthy, loving, supportive relationship in which one feels safe, understood, and embraced for who they are.

This in no way implies that relationships are supposed to be perfect, because even the most compatible partnerships and less dysfunctional families all require significant effort to produce life-giving results. This means that some of these aforementioned issues may arise from time to time, but they are not the dominant part of the relationship. However, I am stating that when you are experiencing frequent and continual encounters that are energy depleting rather than life giving, you are most likely in a toxic relationship.

It is also imperative to note that as significant as the relationships may be with our spouses, romantic partners, parents, and friends, the most important relationship we will ever have is the one we have with ourselves. Wherever we go, there we are. This has two-fold implications, with the first being that what is going on with us internally reflects outwardly in our tangible lives. We must carefully reflect upon the belief system that we have nurtured within ourselves, our own ability to love and be loved, to know our self-worth, to have good self-esteem, and to have the ability to achieve our own hopes and dreams. If we are playing a repetitive negative tape to ourselves, indeed this is a toxic way of relating to ourselves. A toxic relationship with ourselves is destructive where personal growth and development are concerned: it is void of self-love, compassion, and self-acceptance. It is energy depleting and it stunts our ability to flourish. Oftentimes, these self-limiting ideas about ourselves are borne out of past traumatic experiences or the home environment in which we were raised. Nonetheless, it limits our way of being in the world in a way that is healthy and beneficial to ourselves, our families, our communities, and humanity at large.

If we have a toxic relationship with ourselves, naturally it becomes easier to attract relationships with others who are reflective of the relationship we are having with ourselves. As I mentioned in the preface of this book, one of my traumas of parental absenteeism and abandonment during my childhood caused me to create negative tapes about my ability to be loved and wanted by others. This resulted in a series of unhealthy relationships with men over many years, until I continued to explore in greater depth my personal contribution to how my life was unfolding. It was never about the men; the issue was always about the men that *I attracted* and *said yes* to. What I discovered was that I always accepted the level of love I thought I deserved at the time. If I felt I deserved less, less is what I had in my life as a romantic partner.

As I grew in my own self-love and understanding, so did the quality of men I attracted and said yes to immensely improve. Don't get me wrong: there have still been a few strays here and there that have tried to slide into the inner circle of my energetic field, but because I am much more in tune with my self-value, and because I am stronger and wiser, now it is easier to respond to them with an unapologetic "NO!"

Introspection is definitely a key to understanding what role you are playing in your toxic relationships. There are times when we may play the role of the victim (the receiver of toxic behavior from a toxic person), the perpetrator (the one who is demonstrating or giving off toxicity), or even the co-conspirator (someone who is playing a dual role of giving and receiving toxicity within the relationship).

EXAMPLES INCLUDE

You as victim (receiver of toxicity) might experience someone constantly criticizing the things you do; belittling you in front of others; manipulating or guilt-tripping you into doing what they want you to do or getting you to not do things you want to do; controlling your movement, behavior, and actions by not allowing you to make any decisions; exuding intimidating or threatening behavior; alienating you from others; abuse of any kind that includes physical violence, verbal name calling, emotional shutdown or withdrawal, or sexually forcing you into unwanted encounters, positions, or locations.

Perpetrator (giver of toxicity). If you are the one demonstrating any of the behaviors above then you are the perpetrator of the toxicity in the relationship and the other person is the victim (receiver of the toxicity). Other examples of you being the perpetrator could include:

- You are using the person to get what you want from the other person, which could be material possessions, career advancement, and so much more for as long as you can get it.

- You play the passive aggressor by willingly giving all your control and decision making over to the other person so you don't have to be held responsible if a bad decision is made.

- Demonstrating jealously or possessiveness by acting as if there is no room in the other person's life for anyone but yourself and you behave accordingly by displaying some of the other toxic characteristics mentioned because of your inability to accept that the other person's life involves other people.

Co-conspirator. Both you and the person you are in a relationship are mirroring toxic behaviors toward each other. That can be a very destructive place that is physically, mentally, and emotionally exhausting for everyone involved even innocent bystanders. If you were not like this prior to this relationship, then the person you are with has managed to bring out the worst in you instead of your best. There is nothing life giving about being in a relationship with someone who magnifies your darkness and blocks out your beautiful light. You are just as much responsible as they are because the only power they have to bring out your ugly ways is what you give to them. It takes at least two people to be co-conspirators; you are free to make a new choice at any time and therefore change the dynamics of your relationship. When co-conspirators are involved, the relationship can last for decades until one of the parties decides to change, then the toxic scales are no longer balanced.

Regardless of what role you are playing in your relationship toxicity, the only person you are capable of changing is yourself. No matter how often you play the, "if you love me, you will change" card, it ultimately holds very minimum power. People usually only change when there is an internal motivation as the driving force like a paradigm shift in consciousness, spiritual awakening, or expansion in values. Internal changes can be initiated by external factors like a spouse moving out, a life-threatening experience, financial crisis, or other life challenges, but the motivation comes from within. When you go to those you love and ask them to change for you, the change is usually superficial at best and does not last long. Change from within is something that has to be nurtured over time, because when there is an internal desire for change the person can more likely withstand the various obstacles that arise as they are creating healthier behaviors and habits.

When you shift the focus from the other person to yourself in any relationship, especially a toxic one, the situation has no choice but to change because you are changing. As humans in life, we are here to grow and that requires change whether we are ready for it or not; it somehow just happens anyway. Playing any role in a toxic relationship is an opportunity for you to discover what your personal value system is and work on developing a new one that will help you flourish into all you can be in life.

If you are the receiver of the toxicity, a person can only respond to you with words or behaviors that you are choosing every day to accept. This acceptance is conveyed through your continuation to interact in the relationship in the same ways you always have. Any non-working resolution tactics will include anything that does not diminish or eliminate the toxic behavior. You are still there actively participating in giving and/or receiving toxins from your dysfunctional relationship. You cannot change what you don't first acknowledge. Going within to examine and strengthen your core concepts of self and true desires, and redefining who you are and how you want to show up in the world, then beginning to live from that space is what will motivate you toward daily change. As you begin to change, you will begin to attract to you those people who reflect your new attitude about yourself. Toxic relationships and interactions will begin to fall away because your energetic shift no longer welcomes it into your personal space.

You will be empowered by your growth to establish new boundaries and courage to speak up for what your needs are in any relationship. There will be a natural shift toward meeting you where you are in your new conscious awareness, and all who do not get with the new program will naturally fall away just as naturally as when you attracted them to you in the first place. As you grow, unfortunately everyone does not grow with you; preparing yourself to walk away or have the perpetrators walk away from you is usually the healthiest outcome. If the toxic person in your life is remaining stagnant by not being intentional about their own positive growth and development, your newfound self-worth will repel their toxic energy, plain and simple. You will exhaust a greater amount of energy trying to keep a relationship together that has reached this point than you will expel dealing with the emotional pain involved in letting it go.

At this point you may be saying to yourself that this could work for friendships and romantic partnerships, but what about when the toxic person in your life is one or both of your parents? The same rules apply. Your parents will always be who they are until they decide to change; they must be given the freedom to be themselves. If the way they are being is offensive, disrespectful, or abusive to you in any way, you have the power as an adult to choose to exit their line of fire. It is perfectly normal to continue to love and respect your parents but you do not have to interact with them in a way, that is damaging to your own growth and development. Just because your parents were physically responsible for your birth does not mean that you have to accept their own internal battles being any more damaging to your life as they were during your childhood when you didn't have a choice. Sometimes in order to heal your own wounds and become stronger in your boundaries, it is better to show love and respect at a distance; that plays out in different ways for different people.

Desiring attention, connection, affection, communication, and acceptance is a natural response to being human. Having special people in your life who provide you with that level of intimacy should make you feel elevated, safe, secure, cared about, and protected. Intimacy is a shared experience, and if these are not the feelings you experience most of the time when you are interacting in any relationships with family or friends, then it is time to reevaluate your reasons for nurturing and maintaining a connection that is not conducive to your evolution and growth. Freeing yourself of toxic relationships will reduce your stress and free up your life to flourish into all that you were created to be and the relationships you will attract moving forward will be reflective of that.

FIVE WAYS TO FREE YOURSELF FROM TOXIC RELATIONSHIPS

1. Check yourself! Your relationships are mirror reflections of who you are.

2. Improve the quality of the relationships you attract by improving the quality of the relationship you are having with yourself. Be the qualities you desire to experience from others.

3. People can only treat you how you allow yourself to be treated. Establish healthy boundaries of what is acceptable and what is not.

4. Define your own value for yourself in spite of the opinions of others who do not think highly of you.

5. Trust the unpredictability in the freedom of letting go of toxic relationships more than the certainty of painful outcomes of holding on to them.

SECTION SUMMARY

A Day in the Life of Toxic Exposures

Ann was still furious with her husband Rob as she slammed down on her alarm clock. She knew she had exhausted all of her opportunities to snooze, and as it buzzed obnoxiously for the third time, she couldn't fathom how she would muster up the energy to face another long day. She looked over at Rob who still slept soundly and was again resentful of how he had berated her on the phone for nearly an hour yesterday as she maneuvered down the congested expressway to get home. He had once again gotten angry that she had worked late and was unable to prepare him dinner as she'd promised. She had meant to get home at a decent hour, but the required training her boss had unexpectedly mandated, ran late. Once home, she ended up staying up much later than usual to appease him with some "quality time" to make up for her dinner slight. Now, she would have to get through an entire day on three hours of sleep while Rob slept in, not needing to report to his job until much later.

She dragged herself into the bathroom to get ready for work and quickly remembered that she was running low on toiletries. She was so preoccupied with how she would calm Rob down when she got home last night that she had completely forgotten to stop by the neighborhood Dollar Store to replenish her personal care supplies. After relieving her full bladder, she looked in the mirror and disapproved of the generally dull and washed-out reflection that greeted her. She ran her fingers through her dry and brittle hair which was long overdue for a good shampoo. She pulled out a haggard tube of toothpaste that had been cut at the bottom to allow her toothbrush access to the last remnants of paste that hid in the crevices of the empty container. As she listlessly moved the soft bristles against her teeth, she wondered how her life had become this mundane. She hoped a hot shower would help motivate her as she lathered up with what was left of her paper thin bar of soap. As she washed her hair, she was careful not to let too much conditioner drip into her eyes before rinsing it out. The last thing she needed was another contribution to her already bloodshot eyes. After drying off and moisturizing her body, she carefully applied her makeup to mask the prominent bags under her eyes and camouflage the worry lines that had settled into her once even-toned skin. She glanced at her chipped nail polish and promptly decided to opt out of cooking breakfast in order to re-polish her nails and give them sufficient time to dry.

By the time she left home, she was already ten minutes behind schedule. In order to save time and pacify her growling stomach, Ann decided to stop by the corner gas station and pick up a quick breakfast. She grabbed a premade breakfast sandwich from the warmer, the last jelly donut in the display case, and a much needed large coffee with plenty of cream and sugar to jump start her idle brain. She tried to enjoy her breakfast as she squeezed her way into the bumper-to-bumper traffic that again crept along the expressway. She prayed she'd make it to work on time today and avoid another write-up. Though she didn't enjoy her job at the carpet factory, it was currently the only aspect of her life that gave her any reasonable sense of security.

Throughout this section I have listed multiple categories of the most common toxic exposures and some of their associated chemicals. It is clear that within the first couple of hours of waking every morning the average person has already been exposed to a variety of toxic chemicals upon arriving to school or work each day. It is routine to do all of these daily repetitive tasks that include toxic exposures throughout each day, week, month, year, and lifetime, which is what produces a toxic load on the body. This cumulative burden works to support a dis-eased state instead of a "life-supporting" state of being. Every day you are either doing things to support, nurture, or develop the body or you are doing things to help destroy it.

Being cognizant of the plethora of toxins that we are exposed to everyday throughout the day can absolutely feel a bit overwhelming, but wait before you get too discouraged with life and the environment. It is definitely possible to begin or continue to live a full abundant life while experiencing the outdoor elements, eating, drinking, working, and playing. There is always hope because the human body is built to withstand the toxins that are a daily occurrence to life. Having a built-in self-repair mechanism comes with the benefits of not succumbing to life but overcoming its many challenges—this means toxins of all kinds. The silver lining to a life filled with all these toxins can be found in what medical science calls emunctories.

"The best medicine is to teach people how not to need it."
—Unknown

PART 3

DETOXIFICATION PATHWAYS

E MUNCTORIES ARE ORGANS AND PARTS OF THE BODY THAT CARRY OFF waste products. The body has everything it needs to survive and thrive, however it is up to people individually to support that process through a holistic Detox-style. If you are doing more to work against the process, as listed in some of the more controllable toxic exposures listed in previous chapters, then you are encouraging your internal environment to become a breeding ground for disease.

Although you are exposed to numerous toxins throughout the day, humans have various pathway channels throughout the body that are releasing these toxins. There are toxic exposures you can control and those you cannot, but it really comes down to supporting the body's ability to discharge the toxins in equal measure to the amount that you are exposed to them, all throughout the day, each and every day. In the following pages you will learn more about the function of each emunctory and simple ways to support them. Additional information on herbal supplements and other supportive therapies to target specific and general detoxification pathways can be found in chapters 12 and 13.

CHAPTER 10

SUPPORTING THE DETOXIFICATION PATHWAYS/EMUNCTORIES

Kidneys—The urinary system is made up of two kidneys, two ureters, the urinary bladder, and the urethra. This system provides filtration, storage, and transportation for the urine, which is the final waste product that exits the body out of the urethra. *"Every day, the two kidneys filter about 120 to 150 quarts of blood to produce about 1 to 2 quarts of urine, composed of wastes and extra fluid."*[1] The leading role in this uri-

---

1   "Your kidneys and how they work." (May 2014) Retrieved from http://www.niddk.nih.gov/health-information/health-topics/Anatomy/kidneys-how-they-work

nary pathway belongs to the kidneys, which are responsible for processes that impact the body at large. Detoxification is an important part of these processes because the kidneys are filtering waste products and excess water out of the blood, with the end product being urine. When urine is excreted from the body it is also clearing out foreign substances such as drugs and environmental toxins along with other waste products. The quality of kidney function is a strong health indication; therefore, keeping this elimination pathway supported and clear from any obstructions or disruptions is imperative to any cleansing or wellness program. Staying hydrated to maintain fluidity of waste elimination is a primary way to help support kidney function. Drinking water at a minimum of half of your body weight in ounces per day supports this emunctory, in addition to maintaining a normal blood pressure.

Intestines—The intestines are a part of the gastrointestinal (GI) system and are located toward the end of the digestive tract in the body. All of the other organs and organ systems throughout the body are sustained by the healthy function of the GI tract because it is through the GI tract that the body receives the necessary fuel to be energized to do all that is required to sustain itself. Along the GI tract digestion, absorption and assimilation of nutrients is taking place throughout the path completing in the small and large intestines/colon. This is where the body leaves behind all unwanted toxic fecal material to continue to traverse through the remainder of the colon until it is eliminated as a waste product. Because all remaining material in the colon is toxic bacteria-filled waste, it becomes disease forming when left inside of the body for extended periods of time. This waste product ferments and becomes putrid inside the body and is meant to be eliminated. When people experience chronic constipation, it is a result of the body holding on to this toxic waste. I have already established in earlier chapters that having only one bowel movement per day is considered mild constipation, so eliminating only three to four times per week is moderate and one to two times weekly or less is considered severe constipation.

Over time, the colon walls can become impacted and encrusted with an accumulation of fecal matter that has been pushed to the side while a more recent bolus of waste material passes by to get eliminated; this can cause a narrowing of the passageway or blockage. Colorectal cancer is the third leading cancer found in men and women in the United States and the second most common cause of cancer related deaths between both sexes. One of the best ways to prevent this type of cancer and others is supporting the pathways that are designed to eliminate toxins from the body because holding on to the toxins can ultimately have severe consequences. Eating a diet high in fiber rich foods such as: vegetables, fruits, and legumes, exercising, and drinking plenty of water supports this emunctory.

Lungs—The respiratory system is composed primarily of the lungs and a variety of other structures that act as passageways for oxygen to enter the body and oxygenate the blood along with contributing to the aerobic (when the body is moving) and anaerobic (when the body is at rest) metabolic process that takes place during the inspiration of air. Specific to detoxification is the removal of oxygen's waste by-products known as carbon dioxide, which happens during the expiration of air. There is a constant even exchange of this process that goes on naturally without interruption until lung function is compromised by congestion, obstruction, or constricted airways, all of which reduce the lungs' capacities to normally function in its full ability to retrieve and release air. Breathing normally from the diaphragm throughout the day, in addition to practicing deep breathing during yoga or meditation and regular aerobic activity helps to support the lungs.

Lymphatic System—The lymphatic system is a collection of organs that contain lymphoid tissues such as lymph nodes, spleen, thymus, and tonsils that all contain lymphocytes (a sub-type of white blood cells) which support the immune system. Fluid known as lymph is transported from these tissues and throughout the entire body in unidirectional vessels all moving toward the heart. The lymph contains oxygen, nutrients, and hormones in addition to toxic by-products and other waste materials that are eventually filtered through the venous system and eliminated through the other detoxification pathways such as the liver, colon, kidneys, skin, and lungs. Preventing stagnation throughout the body is very important particularly as it relates to the lymphatic system whose circulation is filtering out waste combated by the immune system; it is therefore imperative to health and wellness. The circulation of lymph throughout the body is not driven on a pump system but on movement; maintaining an active body via exercise in addition to a healthy diet and proper hydration are primary ways to support this detoxification pathway.

Skin—As mentioned in the section on toxic personal care products, the skin is the largest organ on the human body that serves as the immune system's first line of defense against foreign invaders known as *pathogens*. The skin protects the inside environment containing our cells, tissues, organs, and organ systems from the outside elements of the world in which we live. The skin has sweat glands embedded in most areas around the human body that excrete perspiration. When we perspire it is the body's natural way of regulating its internal body temperature by cooling itself in addition to releasing waste products out of the body onto the skin via the perspiration. Skin is highly absorbent, therefore many products that are applied to it get absorbed into the bloodstream as a nutrient or a toxin. Supporting skin detoxification can be as simple as participating in activities that will naturally stimulate your sweat glands like exercise and saunas.

Liver—The second largest organ in the body is the liver and it is indeed a powerhouse that functions similar to a shipping and receiving warehouse. The liver receives substances, filters out what nutrients are needed for the body from what is not, and then repackages the unwanted substances as toxic waste products in preparation for them to be excreted from the body via urine or fecal matter. The liver's power does not stop there: it plays a variety of other roles that include acting as a storage unit for bile (needed to digest and absorb fats), glycogen (the stored form of glucose used for energy), and some vitamins and minerals; metabolizes proteins, fats, and carbohydrates; breaks down endogenous (substances made inside the body) and exogenous (substances made outside the body) substances; and processes bile synthesis.

The liver is also responsible for Phase I and Phase II Detoxification, which break down fat-soluble and water-soluble substances and prepares them for elimination from the body. Keeping the liver supported at all times is critical to the health and well-being of the human body because everything is passing through the liver. If there is a stagnation in any of the stored substances being released as needed, metabolized properly, or excreted in a timely fashion, it could potentially lead to other problems throughout the body. These substances can include both nutrients and toxins from the foods and beverages we consume, the medications and supplements we ingest, the hormones our bodies produce, or the external factors to which they are exposed, in addition to a wide variety of other toxic exposures we encounter on a daily basis. You can keep the liver strengthened and tonified to do its job without congestion, limitation, or stagnation by eating a diet rich in dark leafy greens along with cruciferous vegetables such as broccoli and cauliflower and fruits that are packed with antioxidants. Utilizing some of the other natural therapies listed in Chapter 13 and 14 will assist as additional support.

Uterus—This detoxification pathway is primarily applicable to menstruating women only, but all readers can find some value in the information shared. Often referred to as the womb of a woman, the uterus is a regenerating organ that plays a very important role in the progression of humanity. The uterus releases the flow of menstrual blood through the vagina (a canal that acts as a uterine passageway) and it is not commonly referred to as a detoxification pathway. Many women are probably more familiar with hearing that the vagina is a self-cleaning organ. I am not negating this statement, however it is important to reiterate the toxic impact of endocrine disruptors as discussed in chapter 2 along with other toxic factors that interrupt reproductive function. In addition, the vagina's position of being a passageway to and from the uterus, places this orifice in direct contact with a variety of potential toxic exposures. These include: bare penises which carry the risk of sexually transmitted infections (STIs), and penises covered with condoms that have toxic ingredients such as nonoxyol-9. This spermicide is also the active ingredient in other contraceptive foams, gels, and suppositories and its long-term exposure can cause imbalance in vaginal flora. Other direct exposures can include inserted stimulation devices, tampons, along with other personal hygiene products containing endocrine disruptors and other toxic ingredients. It is also important to restate that the body has a built-in self-healing and self-repair mechanism to aid in its ability to release toxins regularly. However, when the body has more toxic exposures to clog up channels and disrupt organ function rather than proper nutrients and outlets that support organ function and cleansing; the reproductive tract will demonstrate symptoms of imbalance.

I have encountered many patients who are enduring very significant imbalances in their reproductive organ function. Women can have varying symptoms of reoccurring vaginal infections (bacterial, viral, fungal/yeast), vaginal odor, discharge, menstrual cramps, irregular menses, and heavy bleeding and will seek out conventional medical care that oftentimes does not completely resolve the issue, especially without manipulating normal function. Unfortunately, many women with these reoccurring imbalances fail to realize it is not another round of antibiotics, antifungals, or synthetic hormones that their reproductive parts are lacking. In many cases, the reproductive tract is crying out for more supportive, tonifying care of natural hormonal balancing, detoxification, and cleansing of the body rather than suppressive treatments from medications.

The reproductive organs collectively function on a regulated cycle driven by a pool of hormones with the largest contributors being estrogen and progesterone. The average female of menstruating age who is not pregnant will experience a menses approximately every twenty-eight days (with some variation in length). When the menses takes place it is the shedding of the endometrial lining of the uterus. During days fifteen to twenty-eight of an average cycle, this lining becomes thick and filled with blood to support a fertilized egg. When there is no fertilized egg the lining thins out and releases the blood in the form of a menses. This cycle is designed to occur ongoing from puberty until menopause with pregnancy being the only naturally causing alteration to adjust function. The reproductive tract operates on an intact hormone feedback signaling system that begins in specific aspects of the brain such as the hypothalamus and anterior pituitary gland and continues down into target organs that include the ovaries, uterus, and vagina that keep this cycle regulated. When the body experiences a disruption or change in its hormonal levels outside of the norm at any level of this feedback system, it can impact the regulation of the menstrual cycle.

When there is an excess or insufficiency of hormones circulating in our bodies that require balance, it affects not only the flow of the menses but also has a direct impact on the entire reproductive environment. This can indirectly affect other organ systems like the nervous system and the endocrine system. The flow of menses frequency, duration, amount, color, and consistency can be strong indicators of the health of a woman's reproductive tract. Science has evolved to a level where we can now manipulate reproductive function by adding synthetic hormones, in the form of patches, vaginal rings, intrauterine devices (IUDs), Depo-Provera shots, and birth control pills. All of these devices have been clinically studied and found to be more than 90 percent effective in protecting against an unwanted pregnancy; however, with every convenience we add to our lifestyle that disrupts the normal flow of our organ systems, there are also risks and consequences involved.

The reproductive tract is a very complex and multilayered topic. My focus on the detoxification of the uterus is intended to provide a surface level of understanding of the importance of discharging blood and fluids from the body that are no longer needed. When we introduce other toxic exposures intentionally in the form of birth control and other aforementioned products, cleansing the reproductive environment becomes necessary to continue to eliminate residues and support the regulation of normal balanced hormonal and organ function. Supporting this detoxification pathway can include numerous ways such as: Kegel exercises, limiting and choosing sexual partners wisely, using condoms outside of monogamous partnerships, and limiting exposure to endocrine disruptors (see Chapter 2). Dietary modifications includes eating a whole foods balanced diet that incorporates fermented foods, iron rich foods, flaxseeds, and cruciferous vegetables, while avoiding sugar and processed soy products.

Mind—This detoxification pathway is different from the other emunctories because all of the other detoxification pathways are releasing waste products. With the mind, its toxicity comes from holding in your purpose, passion, and that which you were created to do. When we hold in our self-expression it becomes toxic to the body on a cellular level. People often say, "What God has for me is for me." That is true on one level but on another level you are here as gifts for the greater good of humanity, you are simply serving as a conduit for that expression to come forth into full manifestation. To hold in those gifts of purpose, creativity, and passion means that they are not being shared with others. Not only do others lose out on benefiting from the transforming gifts you have to offer the world, but you as the individual suffer internally from a constant nagging desire to be your full self, no matter what. That constant nagging desire never goes away because it is fighting to be free on the outside of you. Keeping it trapped inside becomes toxic. There is energy required to harness your internal battle and struggle to suffocate your hopes and dreams, this energy creates the toxins that lead to a slow internal death. Les Brown once said, "The graveyard is the richest place on earth because it is here that you will find all the hopes and dreams that were never fulfilled, the books that were never written, the songs that were never sung, the inventions that were never shared, the cures that were never discovered, all because someone was too afraid to take that first step, keep with the problem, or determined to carry out their dream." Therefore, you must live out those things you were created to express or risk a toxic buildup over time.

What makes this pathway different from the other detoxification pathways is that the gift of expression that comes to you is to be manifested through you. To hold it in is toxic but to release it is the beauty of what it is supposed to become once it is released. Therefore it is not released as a waste product like the other detoxification channels in the body because it becomes life giving and life supporting only when it is outside the body. When surveys were taken of people at the end of their life journey, a larger percentage of seniors had more regrets for the things they did not do in life rather than those things that they did do and possibly failed at.

Although I had spent years enjoying my work in human services and the difference I made to others, the depths of my passion and calling to also serve the physical aspects of health began to deepen annually. The calling grew into a gnawing inside of me to be equipped to help the whole health of people and not just components. As compelled as I felt to help others with their physical health, I allowed my personal challenges with perpetual weight fluctuations to deter me for years from taking the next steps needed to follow my calling. I fought the urge daily with messages that no one would be interested in what an overweight person had to say about health. As time progressed, I had to learn to trust God, myself, and my inner spiritual calling more than I trusted the potential rejection from others. Not only did I finally apply, attend, and complete medical school but I have now written my first book as a testament that God can turn our greatest fears into our greatest triumphs. A calling does not mean the road towards completion will be easy but I can 99¾ % guarantee you, if you stay the course, it will be worth it!

Express life in all of its many forms and allow yourself to be all that you were created to be. That is the best way you can support your mind emunctory in addition to Detox-style practices such as prayer, meditation, journaling, and creative arts expression that are found in chapter 12.

"Let food be thy medicine and medicine be thy food."
—Hippocrates

PART 4

HOLISTIC DETOXIFICATION STEP BY STEP

CHAPTER 11

DETOXIFICATION MEAL TYPES

WHETHER YOU ARE CHOOSING A TIME SPECIFIC DETOX OR A DE-tox-style, dietary control and modifications are going to be pivotal to the success of your cleansing practices. There are foods available that are more disease preventing and life supporting as well as foods that are more disease causing and life taking. Choosing the right foods while participating in a detoxification protocol for a dedicated time period can aid you in cleansing as well as stimulating a desire to begin a Detox-style as a means to support your overall health and well-being. There are a multitude of detoxification and cleansing methods at your disposal via the internet and other resources; however, for the purpose of this book, I will be focusing on three different types that may or may not overlap with other programs. The detoxification and cleansing methods that I use with my patients include hypoallergenic/elimination diet; modified fasting; and fasting, all of which have been very effective because they meet the patient where they are in their willingness and medical ability to commit.

HYPOALLERGENIC /ELIMINATION DIET

For the person brand new to detoxification and fasting, starting out at this level is recommended as you adjust your body to eating a simple yet healthy diet that will help it cleanse. Staying consistent and committed throughout the length of time you have selected to detox is more important than starting out at a more intense level and not completing the process because your ravishing hunger pangs get the best of you.

This level consists of eating small frequent meals throughout the day that include breakfast, lunch, dinner, and one to two snacks (optional). You should not eat to the point of feeling stuffed but, rather, to the point of satisfaction. Only foods on the consumption list should be consumed, while eliminating all the foods from the avoid list for the duration of the detox. A detailed list of the examples of foods from both sections can be found in chapter 15.

CONSUMPTION FOODS:

CHOOSE ORGANIC-ONLY AND FRESH/RAW/LIVING FOODS AS MUCH AS POSSIBLE

- Vegetables (multiple colors)
- Fruits
- Nuts/Seeds
- Whole grains
- Legumes

AVOID FOODS:

- Dairy
- Eggs
- Sugars/Sweeteners
- Peanuts
- Wheat
- Refined grains (white grains)
- Caffeine
- Fried foods
- Processed and packed food

- Meats/Poultry/Fish

- Sodas

- Concentrated juices

- Alcoholic beverages

You are basically providing for the body all the foods that are closest to their natural states for a specified period of time. The less challenges that your body has in digesting the foods, the more energy it can utilize toward detoxing, which makes eating primarily organic raw vegetables and fruits the most ideal selections (Please refer to Meal Impact on Detox charts in Chapter 14 for more information). The most important step is to begin eliminating all the foods on the avoid list and other modifications can be added on over the course of the detox or perhaps the next time you detox. Using the Hypoallergenic/Elimination Diet can be utilized for the novice detoxifier or as a maintenance level for people who have made advanced decisions about their wellness. Maintaining at this level of eating contributes to a Detox-style that will support ongoing daily detoxification with more intense cleansing practices (such as the upcoming types listed) reserved for specified periods of times. (See chapter 14 for more information).

MODIFIED FASTING

Modified fasting includes taking all the information from the Hypo-allergenic/Elimination Diet and intensifying it. This can be done in a myriad of ways. A couple of examples include eating one meal per day while blending smoothies or juicing for the remainder of the day. The one plant-based meal can be raw or cooked if needed with a stronger focus on raw foods because they are whole, unaltered nutrition with more enzymes. This frees up digestive energy to be utilized for detoxification. Another option is to abstain from eating and drinking anything other than water during certain time periods of the day, such as from dawn to dusk, and then eating one meal. Having a small window of time per day for food exposure gives the digestive track an opportunity to rest and frees up the energy of the body to focus on toxic elimination.

FASTING

Fasting is eliminating the intake of all solid foods and modifying your intake of nutrients to include only liquids such as water, fresh natural juices (not from concentrate), and vegetable broth. Although smoothies are liquefied, it is still fiber filled food that requires more digestion than non-fibrous liquids, therefore it does not qualify as a liquid fast but modified fasting only. Fasting is the most effective way to detoxify the body because you are temporarily relieving the body from the work required to digest the food. It is expending a very insignificant percentage of its energy to process the liquid nutrients, which frees up a larger percentage of its energy to focus on discharging toxins from the body rapidly, without much interruption. It is the same thing when you are mopping the kitchen floor after a meal: most people usually save that for last because all the crumbs are wiped off the counter, and any spillage and drips from cleaning the kitchen have already happened. However, if there are still other activities going on in the kitchen, you have to divide your energy and attention and the floor does not get completely cleaned because new dirt continues to be added on during the cleaning process. Someone will always be walking across the kitchen floor and utilizing the kitchen, but when you clean it, just for that time alone you want to admire that it is clean. The digestive tract is no different: it will always get used but when you clean it, it keeps toxins from building up to a point of being problematic and you can feel the health benefits of being detoxified without being weighed down or distracted by all the extra digestive activity.

The strongest, fastest, and most powerful way to halt, slow down, or reverse the disease process in my medical opinion is through fasting, but it must be approached with both safety and precaution. It is best to consult with your licensed health care provider before proceeding, especially if you have any pre-existing medical conditions and/or are on any pharmaceutical medications. Going into a period of fasting should always be gradual and never immediate. Reducing the types of foods consumed and their amount over a few days will condition the stomach to be more tolerable during the fasting process. This also helps to slow down the rate at which your body is pulling toxins from your cells in comparison to how fast the body can eliminate them. If the toxins are not discharged from the body as quickly as they are extracted from the cells, or if you have an enormous amount of toxic accumulation, the buildup can potentially cause discomforting reactions. These discomforting reactions are referred to as a *healing crisis* because as bad as the detoxification may make you feel for a couple of hours or a couple of days if you are extremely toxic, you must go through the challenge to get to the benefits. As your body is expelling toxins (toxic reactions can apply to any detox, particularly a fasting protocol) some of those symptoms can include:

- Appetite Loss

- Bad Breath

- Body Aches

- Body Odor

- Diarrhea

- Fatigue

- Fever

- Headaches

- Itching

- Nausea

- Rashes

- Runny Nose

- Vomiting

Understanding this potential on the front end will hopefully discourage you from running out to your local drug store to purchase some over-the-counter drugs to make the discomfort go away. The most beneficial thing you can do if a reaction occurs is continue with your cleansing process, drink plenty of fluids, and give your body much-needed rest during the onset of symptoms till they pass. Once again, it is best to consult with a health care provider skilled in fasting and detoxification to be guided correctly through this process.

CHAPTER 12

STRATEGIES FOR SUCCESSFUL HOLISTIC DETOXIFICATION

I HAVE BEEN DETOXING ON A REGULAR BASIS FOR OVER FIFTEEN YEARS and within the past few years my skin has reached a level of which even I must take notice. Not to mention the countless strangers who regularly stop me just to say how great my skin looks. I have better-looking skin at the fabulous age of forty-two than I ever had in my twenties or early thirties, and it is because I cleanse my body on a cellular level on a regular basis. The next time you decide to invest in a facial and a long list of skin cleansing products, try adopting a Detox-style instead; it works from the inside outward. In addition to glowing skin with evened-out skin tones, other detoxification and cleansing benefits can include:

- Improved health conditions

- Reduction in toxic waste

- Cleansed emunctories

- Increased energy

- Better digestion

- Rejuvenated vitality

- Strengthened immune system

- Reduction in mucus and congestion

- Increased mental clarity

- Lighter feeling

- Improved focus

- Improved sense of well-being

- Weight loss

In addition to the aforementioned general cleansing benefits, when fasting in particular, it opens you up to a greater sense of self-awareness. Food oftentimes serves as an anesthesia by its ability to block people from feeling certain emotions to their fullest extent. When fasting, it shuts down the numbness and allows you to feel the rawness of your emotions. As all the blockers are removed you are opened up to a deeper self-understanding. The pathways are now open for an increased level of intuitiveness and a newfound perspective.

STRATEGIES BEFORE BEGINNING A DETOX

1. *Choose an optimal time period to detoxify, which is at the beginning of each season (spring, summer, fall, winter) especially spring and fall because there are a variety of environmental changes taking place in the atmosphere such as seasonal allergens that some people may be sensitive to. A good detox will cleanse out current impurities, strengthen your immune system, and therefore minimize your response to the seasonal changes.*

2. *Consult with a health care provider for medical guidance on your detox; they can help with issues such as special considerations for any pre-existing medical conditions and assistance with selecting which type of detox program is best for you based on your medical condition, medications, or current tolerance level/motivation. They can also assist with information on determining if any of your medications can be decreased or eliminated during the time of your detox to reduce your level of toxic exposure. It is important to utilize a licensed health care professional who is knowledgeable*

of detoxification such as a Naturopathic Doctor or MD that specializes in Functional or Integrative Medicine.

3. *Specify the length of time to detoxify and cleanse—seven to twenty-one days is the typical amount of time in which you will see your best results with the average being about ten days. Whereas consistent intervals of 1-3 days for a maintenance detox can be very effective as well. Over the past decade and a half that I have been fasting, my goal was to work my way up to forty days and do it annually. I reached twenty-one days prior to going away to medical school, and with the rigorous academic demands it was too much of a challenge to commit to such extensive times of not eating. Now that school is over I am building my discipline back up with combination plans of modified fasting for seven days and fasting for seven days. Depending on your detoxification experience, it can be challenging to avoid foods that you normally eat, especially if you are eliminating all solid foods by fasting. The biggest challenge in this process is mentally committing. However once you are mentally on board, it is just a matter of getting through the process one day or one moment at time. Sometimes it just takes a while to mentally embrace the concept in its fullness, which is why it is best to plan it out ahead of time and mentally condition yourself to gear up for the challenge.*

- Don't plan too far in advance; it is easier to keep pushing the date back and never actually committing.

- Avoid scheduling during a series of social engagements, work travel, and holiday activities. The less temptation you are exposed to during your cleanse the better your chances of success.

- Review your calendar for days when your schedule is relatively stable, you know what to expect as it relates to time and energy. Too many variables in your schedule can disrupt the flow of your new dietary changes and it becomes easier to revert back to old habits for meal selections.

- Wrap your detox around a weekend or other regularly scheduled days off to give yourself time spent at home with minimal things to do in a controlled environment; this will help you stay focused on your goals.

NUTRITIONAL AND HERBAL SUPPLEMENTS

Taking nutritional and herbal supplementation in addition to eating right or abstaining from food is also beneficial to achieving optimal cleansing results during your detoxification. Supportive supplements help your body excrete the toxins once they are released from your cells; if not, the toxins will only continue to recirculate in the body and potentially cause more problems. Toxic cellular removal is like pulling the grime off a saucepan or pot so that it is no longer sticking to the surface. However, just like toxins, the work does not end there. It is important to clean the pot out completely; otherwise, the encrusted food is simply free to move from one area of the pot to another, thereby remaining in circulation to contaminate new meals you prepare in that unclean pot. Supplements will aid in this cellular extraction and removal of toxic waste products from the body; nonetheless, before I provide recommendations on the types of detoxification and cleansing supplements, I have first included some considerations to factor in when purchasing any type of supplementation for detoxing or general use.

Consult with a licensed naturopathic doctor, integrative or functional medicine doctor that specializes in herbal therapy before venturing out on your own to make a purchase. These practitioners are knowledgeable in both pharmaceutical drugs and natural medicine, which becomes important when selecting the right combination of nutritional supplements and herbs, their therapeutic dosages, and best name brands to optimize your wellness. I have seen many patients get motivated to make healthy changes and run out to their local health food store and purchase a variety of products they end up not using, discarding, or giving away because of too many pills, ineffectiveness, or loss of interest/motivation.

Receiving the proper guidance before investing in any supplements is advisable because naturopathic doctors, especially, are knowledgeable of pharmaceutical-grade natural supplements that can come in a variety of combinations. This resource will provide patients with customized dosage levels of products that will be the most effective for the results you are seeking. People take supplements to feel the positive effects of its contents; those effects are significantly diminished if the dosage is too low or the absorptivity of the product is low. Depending on the name brand of the supplements you purchase, the level at which the ingredients are absorbing into your bloodstream may or may not be enough to optimize your health. Naturopathic doctors use supplement manufacturers that maintain high quality standards for products produced. These companies have been researched and demonstrate an elevated quality of pure and clean supplementation without all the unnecessary artificial adders and fillers. The level of concentration of the active ingredients in supplements from these manufacturers can be significantly higher than supplements that are found in stores. These pharmaceutical-grade supplements have a stronger and faster potential for effectiveness because of their higher rate of absorptivity. In addition, there is the synergistic component of a variety of herbs working together in one product to enhance the health and wellness of its users; this eliminates the need of purchasing multiple products for a favorable outcome. Naturopathic doctors are trained extensively in how to combine individual herbs and multi-herb products to yield the most beneficial results.

Lastly, if you have pre-existing conditions and are currently taking medications, it is always best to consult with a naturopathic doctor on supplements before making any purchases to prevent any herb-drug contraindications or interactions. This could include those herbs that reduce or compete with the drug's effectiveness, herbs that may affect the rate the drug is metabolized in the body, or herbs that cause a negative reaction when combined with certain pharmaceutical drugs. On the positive side there are also herbs that can increase the effectiveness of your medication, as well. Therefore, make the investment in your health and well-being by scheduling an appointment with your licensed naturopathic doctor to obtain the navigation you need to make the most optimal supplement purchases.

COLON CLEANSING

An effective colon cleansing product is just as foundational to a good detoxification program as the dietary modifications you make. The role of the colon cleansing product is to bind up toxic waste and eliminate this contaminated fecal material from the body. When consulting with your health care provider about the best supplements and combinations available for you I would recommend the following general guidelines:

1. Colon cleansing products should include natural ingredients that draw toxins and old fecal material out of colon walls. *Key ingredients to consider can include: activated charcoal, bentonite clay; psyllium husk, and pectin powder.*

2. Colon cleansing products should also include natural herbs

that will help to stimulate peristalsis (movement of waste material throughout the GI tract). *Key ingredients to consider can include aloe vera leaf; barley root bark; cascara sagrada; ginger root; and senna.* These ingredients should not be taken on a continual basis; otherwise it will cause your bowels to become lazy, which affects its normal function of peristalsis that generally occurs without stimulants.

3.   For greatest effectiveness product should produce formed fecal matter and not watery content.

4.   Products should not cause any GI disturbances such as abdominal cramping, bowel urgency, or incontinence.

In the past I have used a long list of different products on the market to help me with colon cleansing during my periods of fasting. It took a few years and a lot of trial and error before I found the right combination of herbs to do the most effective job of getting out the old fecal material from my colon walls. You can avoid this exploratory step by visiting your naturopathic doctor for best recommendations. After fasting for fifteen days and using other colon cleansing products, I finally found the right combination of herbs that demonstrated the most optimal results for me. During the last six of my twenty-one-day fasts, I was having four to five full bowel movements per day. I could not believe it because I had not eaten anything for over two weeks but it was apparent by the shape (it was released as a similar shape with indentations as if it were pulled from the cracks and crevices of my colon wall), odor (which was unlike anything I had smelled before) and color (it was much darker like it was really old waste) that this was fecal material that had been accumulating in my body for a long time and it never had the opportunity to fully be eliminated.

At the time of this thorough elimination, I had been detoxifying for years and I considered myself to have normal regularity but no results like this had ever occurred before then. The funny thing is that all throughout my marriage, my ex-husband used to tell me I was so "full of sh*t." Every time he was upset with me or my response to something he would soon follow with that statement. Well if *I was* so full of sh*t; his foolish behavior must have been oat bran because that is what he fed me most of the time. Now you see why I had to divorce him: I was tired of walking around feeling bloated from all that oat bran. However, after my first encounter with this combination of herbs, I had to shamefully admit, he was right—literally speaking, that is. I was simply amazed at all the old fecal matter I was releasing from my body and my most prevailing thought every day was, *What if I had never taken the time to detoxify myself in this way?* Although I was already committed to detoxification and doing more things to support my health than destroy it, I understood more clearly than ever before the necessity to cleanse regularly for optimal health.

Liver Support—I have mentioned in previous chapters how the liver is the powerhouse organ responsible for a multitude of functions throughout the body including Phase I and Phase II Detoxification. This lends credence to the benefits of providing the liver with supplements that will help bile flow, release toxins, protect it from oxidation, and ultimately strengthen and tonify it, all of which will help ensure that the liver has the necessary support to do its job without stagnation or disruption of flow. *Key herbal ingredients to consider can include: artichoke fruit leaf; dandelion root; milk thistle; and turmeric root.*

Kidney Support—The kidneys filter the waste products and additional fluids from blood so that it can eliminate them from the body. Taking a supplement to support this detoxification pathway will help stimulate the kidneys to do their tasks of cleansing in addition to strengthening and tonifying these vital organs for optimal function. *Key herbal ingredients to consider can include corn silk; cordyceps mycelia; and dandelion leaf.*

Uterine Support—At the center of the reproductive organ system is the uterus and keeping it cleansed, strengthened, tonified, and hormonally balanced supports the overall environment. Many herbal supplements for the reproductive area are best consumed during specific times of the reproductive cycle, so it is best to consult with your health care provider for information on dosing for optimal results. *Key herbal ingredients for general tonification herbs can include dong quai; blue cohosh, false unicorn, motherwort, horsehound, or wake robin.*

Probiotics—probiotics are strands of good bacteria that support a healthy gut flora through keeping the digestive tract balanced with the bad bacteria. When you are doing a detox it is important to replenish with a probiotic. When using colon cleansers, especially the most effective ones, all of the bacteria, both good and bad are being flushed out. Therefore, it becomes necessary to repopulate the gut with good bacteria. Steady probiotic support is needed on an ongoing basis even beyond a detox especially if you eat mostly conventional (non-organic) produce because the good bacteria is at risk of being destroyed by the pesticides before those items arrive to the grocery store. That means you are not getting multiple sources of good bacteria while having an abundance of exposures to bad bacteria. It's important to repopulate the gut to support balanced flora, particularly if you have an extensive history of taking antibiotics, which will create a dysbiosis or imbalance between your good and bad gut bacteria. For general maintenance of good bacteria you can also eat fermented foods such as dairy-free yogurt (i.e., coconut yogurt), sauerkraut, miso, tempeh, and drink kombucha tea to name a few.

STRATEGIES TO TAKE DURING A DETOX

Water—Staying hydrated by drinking half of your body weight in ounces of water is very important. The water is acting as a lubricant to help get the fecal matter out of your bowels; otherwise, without the water the contents are dry and become difficult to move through the bowels to the point of elimination. Good hydration also helps your kidneys eliminate waste products via the urinary tract. The best approach is to carry a large stainless steel or glass water bottle with you to drink from throughout the day. Refill as needed, and it will help you monitor how much water you have consumed. The best water types for detoxification includes distilled and alkaline that should be used for short-term use only not exceeding fourteen days. Other water selections that are preferred for ongoing daily usage over a lifetime include purified filtered water such as reverse osmosis or carbon block systems, and spring or mountain spring water.

Herbal Teas—Consuming decaffeinated organic herbal teas such as green, peppermint, or lemon ginger tea can help with bad breath that may occur as well as settle any abdominal discomfort from the detox.

Bowel Movements—Daily bowel movements are an ABSOLUTE necessity while detoxing and doubly important if you are fasting. You must have at least one bowel movement per day; your cells are releasing toxins, and those toxins must be eliminated from the body. Otherwise, they will be released in the bloodstreams and continue to circulate throughout the body, thereby causing a detoxification reaction and other potential harm. If you are fasting there is no food helping to push these toxins out, which is why you need a product to help create the bulk needed to pull and peristalsis assistance to push the toxins and other collected waste materials that have accumulated on the colon walls completely out. Therefore, utilizing the proper supplementation or other colon irrigation techniques, which are listed under the Hydrotherapy section in Chapter 13, becomes a required component of the detoxification process.

Sleep—Obtain eight to ten hours of sleep per day during your detox, depending on if your work schedule can accommodate it. Anything less than six hours is just not sustainable for the healing and restoration that your body is doing during this time of cleansing. Sleeping in on the weekends or non-working days to make up for some of the hours missed during working days can also be helpful.

Sleep acts as a restorative agent doing behind-the-scenes work to prepare you with the energy you will need for the following day. Cellular self-repair of tissues and cells along with continual growth and development are all connected with the process of sleep. Therefore, without adequate amounts of rest we are not giving the body adequate time to fully regenerate. When you sleep your body is still working to repair tissue and cells. That is why when you wake up in the morning you should feel refreshed because your body has spent the past several hours working without interruption to heal and replenish cells to get you ready for all the work you will do the following day. If we are not giving our bodies the opportunity to shut down and go through the restorative process, the cumulative effects become damaging to our health. The need to restore energy is similar to your cell phone battery that depletes according to time and usage. An example would be when the energy capacity in your phone is maxed out and you only have time to charge it up to 27 percent. This allows you to perform some minimal activities that include brief calls, texts, photos, or updating your Facebook status.

After doing all that you may get an important lengthy call that drains the remaining battery charge down to zero. Once you receive notification that the battery is getting low you can charge it up immediately or allow your phone to automatically shut off once all the power is gone. Unfortunately for us, we were not created with any bells, whistles, other sound indicators, or monitors to tell us just how much energy is left in our body before we are forced to recharge. We may not have any audible or visual monitor indicators. But we do have our senses (how we feel, think, and move). As we fight to stay awake we override those indicators with a caffeinated stimulant such as coffee, tea, pills, or bottled energy shots. When the body is fatigued it is not stimulants that it needs, it is rest. To continue to override the system you are denying it of what it needs to self-repair and self-replicate. Rather, that is self-destruction. To use our bodies all day, every day, is to make constant withdrawals from the energy bank; during a good night's sleep, we get to deposit all of what we took out. By providing the body with superficial energy we promote an additional withdrawal. Not giving the body adequate rest means you are not cellularly replacing what was lost in your energy exertion throughout the day. What this equates to is a perpetual deficit because you are making more withdrawals without enough deposits to cover your need for a balanced energy budget. The cumulative impact of a body not self-repairing is a body continually self-destroying and that gives rise to disease in the body. American society has made being busy all the time look glamorous. The rise in health care expenses and diminished quality of life should not be the life we are striving daily to build by boldly neglecting our need for sleep and restoration by proudly proclaiming, "I can sleep when I die."

Exercise—If you are fasting you should not be exercising at all because you are not taking in any food, which means that your body is not receiving enough calories to support the caloric loss to endure the exercise. Excercise will also increase your desire to eat to replenish the supply of energy that has been lost. If you are doing the elimination diet, participating in a moderately paced aerobic activity for at least thirty minutes per day 5 days per week followed by at least five minutes of stretching will help to keep your body fluid and active. Attending yoga classes and doing strength training are other beneficial forms of exercise to participate in while doing this basic level of cleansing.

These physical activities promote the detoxification channels via breathing, sweating, bowel motility, and improved flexibility and motility. Remember to use a towel to frequently wipe sweat off of your body so that toxins in sweat will not reabsorb back into the skin. In addition, rehydrate every 15 minutes to replace fluids lost via sweating. Please consult with your health care provider before beginning any new exercise programs.

MENTAL, EMOTIONAL & SPIRITUAL DETOX STRATEGIES

Avoid Television—Television is filled with excessive food commercials for the latest value meal deal, the new smothered, covered burger that you absolutely must try, and the current sale items at your local grocer. If you are abstaining from the normal foods that will typically show up in these commercials, and especially if you are fasting from food in general, watching television can sabotage your ability to stay committed to the duration of your detox. Typically the happiness and coolness displayed in commercials is being sustained by the latest pharmaceutical drug advertisements that immediately follows the fast food commercials. We have all seen these pharmaceutical commercials and they normally end with a long list of side effects that come from taking the drugs. Like I said, those consumers are not happy and cool for too long.

Oh, but wait, there is some hope if you keep watching, your particular medication might be among the many against which lawyers are building a class-action law suit because of the life-threatening "newly discovered" side effects. Therefore, you may be sick for the rest of your life, but at least you can collect some money from your life-altering side effects. Although, you may not be able to actually enjoy the money after succumbing to all the aches and pains, additional medications, lab tests, and frequent doctor visits to monitor your condition. But hey, you were able to feel happy and cool for a little while at least.

These same commercials stay on a regular rotation, repeating themselves ad nauseam during your one-hour program. During a detox, the value you receive from abstaining from television for several days will far exceed the value you will get from watching TV for any amount of time during the detox.

Outside of fleeing from the many food temptations found on television, replacing the time you would be watching television with spiritual exercises will yield significant rewards. As I mentioned earlier, when you are fasting or detoxifying your body, you are removing clutter not just from your body but your spirit as well. You don't have the same distractions that a fully weighted down stomach trying to digest a multitude of heavy foods will bring. You intuitiveness opens up, and it becomes an opportunity for you to have a heightened sense of awareness about yourself, your environment, your life, your goals, your desires, your needs, your challenges, and your outlook.

As you toss the trashy toxins out of your body, toss them out of your mind and spirit as well. Detoxify those negative and self-sabotaging behaviors and attitudes; excuses about why you cannot achieve your goals; poor habits of putting yourself last on your list; people/things you are unwilling to let go of that no longer serve a purpose in your life, and feelings of resentment toward yourself and others.

When you clean out your colon there is a smoother, easier passageway for future eliminations to flow right on through without obstruction or stagnation. It is just the same when you clean out the pathways of your mind: there is more clarity to make better more life-enhancing decisions because you not only feel what you feel more strongly but you also do not have the mental clutter blocking your level of understanding and ability to more thoroughly process the information.

In my opinion, watching television hinders the depth of this process from happening and it hinders your ability to completely optimize the spiritual, mental, and emotional benefits of detoxification. Nonetheless, if you absolutely must turn on the television, use this time of detoxification and cleansing to review documentaries on health and wellness, motivational speeches, and other positive materials that are going to impact your mind, body, and spirit in a way that is inspiring, uplifting, educational, and purifying. While you are releasing the bad toxins from your body, it is fertile ground for positive information to be infused so that a more beneficial harvest can be reaped.

B ELOW IS A LIST OF OTHER ACTIVITIES YOU CAN DO TO NOT ONLY REplace television but implant into your being those things that will further detoxify and enrich your mind, body, and spirit in ways beyond what you thought were possible. These are all great practices to do on a regular basis for lifetime health improvements; however, during a detox and especially a fast, the benefits of these practices can be maximized substantially.

Meditation—There is great power in quieting the often rampant thoughts of your mind. It does not matter what type of meditation you do—breathing, transcendental, sound, chakra, a yoga combination, or the various other types that are available—it is important to just do it. Although there are a variety of ways in which one can meditate, at the foundation of meditation is being mentally still, focused, open, and quiet enough to simply allow yourself to just be. In those moments of meditation you are relaxed; when you are relaxed your body can focus on self-restoration. Therefore, you are providing the body with sacred time and space to naturally flow toward a life-giving, life-building process. Ripping and running all day on the job, errands, chores, commitments, obligations, and family responsibilities have become the new "normal" for many people who wish there were thirty hours to each day instead of the regular twenty-four. Unfortunately, for these people they are not seeking to add in more time to their day for rest but more time to work and get other things done. This is exactly why meditation is needed. We place a five-page laundry list of activities on our physical and mental/emotional selves every day that we are consumed with from the moment our eyes open each morning until we retire to bed at night. The average body is designed to be very robust, so it is more than capable of doing absolutely everything that we need to accomplish all of our daily tasks.

Nonetheless, if we spend all day taking from the body with all of our many demands to perform, it becomes imperative to participate in some activities throughout the day to give back to the body so that it can have what it needs to get us through the next set of tasks.

Directions for meditating: If you are new to meditating, start with five minutes and add one additional minute per day, working up to at least fifteen to twenty minutes. Plan to meditate twice daily, preferably in the morning upon waking and at night right before bed. Set your timer on your phone or other device before beginning. Begin with sitting in a relaxed position, eyes closed and take five deep breaths, breathing in through the nose and holding for three seconds and releasing out the mouth with an "ahhh" sound after each breath. Continue with breathing normally and allow your thoughts to be still. It takes some discipline to get your thoughts to just stop so each time your mind goes on a tangent about anything choose a word like, "love," "joy," or "peace" to re-center the mind as a gentle command to stop thinking; you will have to do this over and over again for many sessions and, hopefully, the intervals in which you have to do it will grow longer and longer as you retrain your mind to simply exist without thoughts. Dump the thoughts out of your mind and embrace the fullness of what it means to be still, be clear, and just be.

Prayer—It does not matter what religion you belong to or if you even belong to a religion, the divine universal energy source of all that is (I call this source God) is available to everyone regardless of how you came to know this divine energy. When we pray we are getting in touch with that higher divine energy source of unconditional love, everlasting joy, and eternal peace; this source is perfect, whole, and complete in and of itself. All of creation was brought into being from this energy source, which means that the same characteristics of this energy are in each and every one of us. If God is the ocean, we are the water in a glass that represents the human body that physically contains the water that represents the essence of the larger body of substance from which we derived. If God is perfect love, joy, and peace then we embody those same characteristics. As we pray to God, it is an opportunity for us to align ourselves with the essence and the characteristics of this energy source being our essence and characteristics as well, even if we are not living from that place of knowingness. To pray is to center ourselves into oneness with who we truly are, who we were created by God to be: men and women who live and build a life built on love, joy, and peace. The love, joy, and peace inside of us wants us to live a life of greatness, abundance, and fullness, not one of anger, fear, jealously, deceit, greed, resentment, sadness, or maliciousness.

If you don't know what to pray or how to pray, it's as simple as this: become quiet and still and say either to yourself or out loud (out loud is much more powerful) "Divine Source of all things, you are love, joy, peace, creative, and abundant; you created me out of your likeness; therefore, I am love, joy, peace, creative, and abundant. I choose every day in every way to live from this truth about myself. I thank you for the knowledge and acceptance of this truth, and I release it as already being so. Amen." Saying this prayer daily will begin to affirm to you who you really are and your life will begin to shift in powerful and magnificent ways.

JOURNALING

GRATITUDE LIST

Starting and/or ending each day with a list of five things for which you are grateful helps to keep your mind centered on positive things and all the aspects of your life that are working for your benefit (even if it is challenging to see sometimes, all things are working for our benefit even the hardships and trying times). Even if you begin with something as basic as being grateful for your health—you can breathe, walk, put on your own clothes, you can understand the words on this page, you can remember, you can smell, your heart is beating to keep you alive, your lungs are giving you air all throughout each day, and your stomach is digesting your food. You can also be grateful for your family and friends that you get to visit, communicate, and support while also receiving love and support. You can be grateful for the sun that rose this morning, the kind person that let you go ahead of him or her at the grocery store, or the stranger who said hello with a pleasant smile. The list of all the simple things in life that we can be grateful for is endless if we stop long enough to pay attention and give thanks. The more we are thankful for, the more opportunities show up in our lives for us to be grateful, because now we are walking around looking for those positive things and, as we seek them out, they appear.

THOUGHT PROCESSING

In addition to starting and/or ending the day with gratitude, journaling about other specific events that occur throughout the day can help you process information and put things into a perspective of understanding the lessons of challenging situations. Writing out your hopes, visions, dreams, and goals for life is a very powerful tool. You also want to include what your motivations for achieving or accomplishing these goals or visions are (building a better life for yourself and your family, giving back to humanity, or increasing abundance).

Putting your ideas in written form is a very important step in getting on the path toward a better place than where you currently are. Even if you are in a good place in life this is still a useful tool because as long as we are breathing we should be growing. When you write out the larger goals and visions, it will begin to inspire you to consider what steps might be involved in the achievement. Considering that you do not know what you do not know, spending time researching or talking to others who have done something similar is a good way to learn more about the steps involved. As you get familiar with the steps, and write out the process of moving toward your goals, this would be called the plan of action. Remain unattached to the final outcome; be prepared for things to change. How you attain your goals will not be a linear process, as there will be some forks in the road, detours, bumpy bridges, and dark tunnels. The important thing is to stay the course. You will get to a better place within yourself with resilience and hard work that oftentimes requires more strength than you thought you had to give. It is important that you begin and begin it now!

I must warn you: once you write these positive goals down, whether you decide to bring them to reality or not, your life will never be the same. Those positive things you wrote down are seeking to be expressed in reality, and you are the conduit through which they are to come forth to be shared with the world. Go ahead and write them down. Use them as reference tools to stay focused and present to what you are here to do and, ultimately, who you are here to become.

FORGIVENESS

More often than not, before we can truly move forward in our personal growth and development we must first revisit our past emotional hurts, wounds, and traumas. It is helpful to write these events down on paper as we remember them and then follow up with the false belief systems and mental story we told ourselves as a result of the experience happening, as a prelude to the forgiveness journey.

An example of that would be when I mentioned in the preface of this book that one of my traumas was the absenteeism of my mother and the complete abandonment of my father. Because neither of my parents were consistently a part of my daily life, the story I created for myself was that I was not worth loving or getting to know, and I had built a life around that story for decades that overlapped additional traumatic episodes. This included a couple of abusive episodes from another parental figure who, unbeknownst to him, reinforced my story of feelings that I was unlovable and unworthy two times over.

As a result I can honestly say that my journey of forgiveness of those whose responsibility it was to parent me has sometimes felt like climbing a smoothly paved mountain: impossible to do. As I have grown and matured throughout life, my adult self is highly functional and moving forward; I am incredibly intentional about not allowing those feelings to linger because they do creep up often and at what seems like the worst of times. To nurture those feelings about myself will only invite more of those experiences into my world to prove to me that I am right about being unworthy of love, and I do not want to go down that road again. I have to choose to positively reinforce my true nature to myself so that I can experience more of that into my life.

The truth for me is that I was a beautiful child inside and out and I AM an awesome and amazing woman worthy of love and worthy of getting to know. It is unfortunate that my mother, father, and other parental figure missed out on much of this time, but my maternal grandparents, who raised me, certainly gave me the love, attention, and the nurturing I needed to build a foundation to thrive. As much as I love my grandparents and appreciate how they stood in the gap of my absentee parents while they lived their lives independent of me, I could not help but notice the lack of my parents' day-to-day presence and participation in my upbringing and the void I still feel with no memories of ever being at the center of their lives. As much as my grandparents loved me like I was their own, they still had to divide their time, attention, and resources amongst their host of other children and grandchildren. My long-term emotional damage did not occur from the events themselves but, rather, *the story I created about myself* as a result of those events happening. A negative story I held on to for decades. Although my adult self is coping and telling a new story it is the child within me that continues to carry the true depths of this pain.

I share all of this to say that it is critical that forgiveness starts with us. Honor and acknowledge every bad, negative, foul, hurtful, or painful thought about yourself that you have had, the people/persons involved, and the event/s that occurred surrounding the challenging experience by writing it all down. Forgive yourself for accepting lies about yourself from you and others; forgive yourself for repeating the lies to yourself about who you really are.

Now, tell yourself a new story, tell yourself the truth from that part of your being that has never been violated, that part of you that knows there is a divine energy source that created you out of its own image and likeness—one of love and peace (as for me, there is nothing loving or peaceful about believing I am unlovable). Tell yourself a new story about yourself that is filled with self-love, self-acceptance, self-worthiness, self-compassion, and the greatness that you really are.

After you have begun the journey of forgiveness for the stories you have told yourself, you must then admit any dark truths about whatever role you may have played that contributed to the hurtful or painful events unfolding in your life. This is not always the case but in those situations where they are, it is important to own up to your own actions and behaviors. I want to be clear that this does not minimize or change the fact that someone else has deeply hurt you or caused you pain, it simply puts the experience in perspective to open up the necessary channels of healing. Keep at the forefront that you are not your mistakes; if you have wronged someone in the past in isolated instances what you did was a bad thing but it does not make you a bad person. Forgive yourself for the role (if any) that you played in how the hurtful event played out.

Now that you have done your personal work surrounding what initially may have seemed like an unforgivable act, it is time to forgive the other person. Doing the truthful work on yourself first definitely helps to reduce the velocity of the painful blow to your emotions, but it is still painful nonetheless. This final piece of the forgiveness work is not for the other person, it is for you to let go of and begin to heal. It has often been said that not forgiving someone is similar to you drinking a cup of poison and sitting back and waiting for the other person to die. People that have brought you hurt and pain may not think twice about it and have since moved on with their lives while you are left walking around being hurt, angry, and weighed down by what they had said or done, all the while reliving and recreating the event years and sometimes even decades after it had occurred. It was one post out of a thousand on the other person's Facebook timeline and you have created an entire website about the incident that you update regularly. Seriously, it's time to start healing and let it go.

Understand that the deeper the relationship, the deeper the cut, which means the deeper the pain and oftentimes the longer it takes to truly heal. When you have been deeply hurt by someone you love, admired, respected, and had or wanted a close relationship with saying *I forgive you* is only words. But those words put you on the journey of becoming a forgiver of that person—the final destination of forgiveness might be a plane, train, automobile and boat ride across the widest sea. The art of becoming means that it will be a process in getting there; you don't just magically arrive because forgiving is the "right" thing to do. When forgiveness is needed, it more often than not accompanies a trust that has been broken or violated in some way, shape, or form, and re-building trust does not come easy, especially after it has been dismembered in a violent way.

Forgiving others can happen in the form of confronting the person face to face about what happened, writing the person a letter and making sure they receive it, or writing a letter that you never send off because the person may be deceased or unreachable. In some cases it is better to let sleeping dogs lie and not open up any lines of communication. Forgiveness is not contingent upon how or if the other person responds at all or in a way that you deem favorable. The most important thing here is that you do the work for *you*. Some relationships you want to redeem and some are not worth saving at all; regardless, forgiveness is still work that has to be completed to free yourself.

Seeking out other books, resource materials, and therapeutic counseling from certified professionals are means you can utilize to help you navigate your work of forgiveness. I would be lying to you if I told you that this forgiveness component of the cleansing process is easy; in fact, for many, this may be the most challenging aspect in this entire book. I am clear about its contributions to the roots of my on again, off again affair with weight fluctuations. As challenging as you may find this component, do not ever stop working through the process because, I cannot emphasize enough, what begins at the mental/emotional aspect of your health will manifest in the physical. Every aspect of your vitality is equally as important as all the others.

Creative arts expression (visual, performance)—If you are a creative artist, use this time to create something new, get in touch with those creative forces within yourself to express that which is inside of you that seeks expression. Dance, sing, paint, write, compose, speak, act, draw, produce: just release with passion and freedom that which is seeking to be shared through you, outside of you. Make it tangible.

For those of you who are not in touch with your creative side and you do not feel inspired by any creative expression coming forth through you, it is the perfect time to go take a painting lesson, participate in a pottery making class, or line dancing class. If you still are just not that interested, simply go appreciate the creative work of others by visiting a photo gallery, museum, art gallery, theater arts performance, or listening to some live music or spoken word/poetry in an intimate setting. Be inspired, empowered, motivated by the creative expressions taking place to live the kind of life you were created to live. Embrace the freedom and passion of these artists and make it your own to test the limits you have placed on your own life and remove the boundaries that have kept you where you are and instead get propelled toward where you truly want to be in life.

STRATEGIES FOR ENDING DETOX MEALS

HYPOALLERGENIC/ELIMINATION DIET

Once you have ended the dietary regime for this detox and you decide to resume eating your normal diet
1.   Reintroduce small-portion meals throughout the day.

2.   Keep meals simple without consuming more than two different foods from the avoid list during each day (limit meals to one serving of a protein, vegetable, and starch or whole grain).

3.   Wait at least two days before adding two more new foods from the avoid list back into your diet.

4.   As you are slowly reintroducing foods from the avoid list back into your diet, pay close attention to any changes that may occur in your

   •   Bowel habits (are you eliminating more, less, or the same?)

   •   Digestive disturbances (bloating, gas, acid reflux, belching, or abdominal pain)

   •   Congestion or mucus buildup

5.   Eliminate or significantly reduce the consumption of the foods you have identified that are possibly triggering an adverse reaction. Consult with your Naturopathic Doctor for further instructions.

MODIFIED FASTING AND FASTING

Committing to end these levels of detox properly is just as important as you committing to beginning a detox. It is important to remember that you have been using your digestive tract at a very minimal level throughout the duration of your detox, so it must be slowly awakened, not abruptly with a large amount of food to digest at one time. After withholding solid foods and regular meal intervals from the body for an extended period of time, the natural desire, especially if you are new to fasting, is to want to make up for the lost time of abstaining from meals. As a way to keep the desires of the mind occupied, many people will begin to plan out the meals they will have once the fast is complete, and it usually involves an all-you-can-eat buffet or a list of their favorite foods or restaurant spots. This is a huge mistake and strongly discouraged.

1. Plan out your specific ending date of the detox before beginning and commit to sticking to the process for the full duration to avoid abruptly ending due to an uncontrollable urge for food.

2. Retrain your brain to use positive language regarding your abstinence from food. Avoid starvation language. Anything in life is 90 percent mental. This includes your success with completing the detox. If you can mentally accomplish it, the rest is just staying focused and going through the daily process of doing the steps. This is a lot easier said than done, but it is absolutely possible to attain, one moment at a time.

3. End the fast with one to two servings of raw, juicy, fibrous fruit such as an apple, orange, or pear. Chew slowly and enjoy each and every bite. After a period of abstaining from foods this should taste heavenly. Continue to enjoy fresh fruit for snack time as well.

4. Keep portion sizes small for all subsequent meals.

5. For lunch and dinner of Day 1 enjoy a fresh green salad topped with a few vegetables and a light vinaigrette for dressing.

6. On Day 2 follow the same regimen as listed in two and three, however you can add a plant- or animal-based protein to

103

lunch and for dinner you can substitute the salad for some steamed vegetables, legumes, and brown rice.

7.   Continue to keep portion sizes small over the next seven days.

DETOX MAINTENANCE

Detox monthly for one to three days; this can be done for a full day, a weekend, or by shutting off eating at a certain time period through the day. I must add that stuffing your stomach beyond capacity for lunch and then waiting until breakfast the following day before you eat again is NOT a fast or detox. It is you giving your body ample time to digest a very heavy meal. When detoxing or fasting for short or long durations, the key is to eat from the recommended foods list and keep it light. In Chapter 14 you will learn more about detox maintenance and how to implement regular practices into creating your own Detox-style.

CHAPTER 13

SUPPORTIVE DETOXIFICATION THERAPIES

THE FOLLOWING THERAPIES LISTED BELOW ARE FOR GENERAL KNOWL-edge only that should be used in conjunction with a detoxification consultation with a medical professional. Please consult your physician for possible health contraindications before trying any of the listed therapies at home or in a wellness facility.

HYDROTHERAPY

Colon Hydrotherapy (Colonics)—This involves infusing water into the rectum to extract fecal material from the colon. Obtaining a series of colonics (a minimum of three consecutive colonics; for optimal benefits continue for up to three weeks) will be the most effective use of this time of colon irrigation during a detox. I recommend a series within a minimum of one week because each colonic is building on the work of the previous one. With each irrigation the water is loosening up more waste material that has been impacted on the colon walls and is capable of reaching further up the colon after each session. Therefore you do not want too much time to pass before continuing with the series. Hence, obtaining only one colonic is not going to be very beneficial, especially if your current bowel movement occurrences are less than one time per day. Maintaining the benefits of a colonic after the initial series with a tune-up colonic once every three to four months will help to keep the colon supported to detox.

Ultimately what this colon irrigation should be doing is supporting the body's natural ability to eliminate waste on its own. By removing old fecal matter and deeply encrusted impaction from the colon walls, it creates more room for the passage of waste products without any obstructions to the fluidity of its movement. Utilizing colon hydrotherapy in combination with a detoxification diet or fasting will provide the most optimal benefits for your body. The goal is to remove barriers to self-repair and not replace function; therefore, combining a healthy diet with the colonics will not only remove old waste material but remove barriers for the body to more freely eliminate toxic waste from your body on its own. Colonics can be obtained at wellness facilities that offer colon hydrotherapy as a service. Colema/Colonic boards can also be purchased online for self-administered colon hydrotherapy with effects that are middle of the road between a health spa colonic and an at-home enema (see below).

Enemas—Enemas are a much more simplified version of the colonic; this means that it does not have the pressure or the far-reaching power of the colon irrigation and it can be done in the privacy of your own home. To extend the reach of the enema it is better to invest in a quart-size enema bag instead of the standard 4.5-ounce pre-made enema bottles that can be purchased at your local drug store. These are fine in case of an emergency to remove waste material that is sitting in your rectum (just above your anus) and you need an immediate release without much thought, planning, or practice involved. However, if you are planning a detox it is best to go to a medical supply store and purchase a reusable 2.5-quart-sized transparent enema bag in addition to a six-inch catheter to attach to it. This size will be much more beneficial in loosening up fecal matter so that it can assist you in moving your bowels. These can be done during the time of a detox but not on a regular basis. Once again the goal is not to replace colon function but to support it for a specified period of time in order to improve independent function supported by ongoing hydration and a healthy, clean diet. If the peristalsis (the muscle contraction that propels digested bulk forward through the digestive tract) in the colon is not being utilized it will stop working independently, therefore you can create a dependency on enemas. Use of enemas should be in conjunction with a fasting/detoxification program and should not extend past twenty-one days.

Vaginal Steam (Also known as a Hip Bath, V-Steam, or Yoni Steam)—This ancient vaginal hydrotherapy that is emerging in the Western society is designed to cleanse, tonify, and improve circulation of the vagina and uterus by exposing it to steamed herbs specific to supporting hormonal balance and overall reproductive function. This involves sitting without any undergarments on a seat that has an opening in the middle (similar to a toilet seat) so that a pot of hot water infused with dry herbals roots, petals, and leaves releases their volatile oils (the medicinal parts of the plants). A drape encloses the lower portion of the body with the seat and pot underneath to lock in the heat and moisture as the gentle medicinal steam travels upward permeating the vagina and the uterus.

Herbal vaginal steams are recommended as part of a complete holistic detox program for women and can be taken in conjunction with oral botanical herbs for increased effectiveness. Consult with your local practitioner regarding possible contraindications to the steam therapy or herbal combinations. Vaginal steams are available at wellness centers, spas, or equipment and supplies can be purchased online for at home therapy sessions. 1-3 treatments per month for 30-45 minutes during a detox and/or for on-going women's wellness support is recommended. This therapy should not be used during your monthly menses.

Sauna/Steam Room—Skin is the largest organ of the body, which is filled with pores that can release sweat and therefore help to detoxify the body. Using a sauna or steam room is another way to help the body produce sweat, thereby releasing more toxins. Many health clubs have steam rooms and possibly a traditional sauna that you can utilize. These traditional saunas and steam rooms provide an external heat in the environment that will make your body produce sweat. Spending three ten-minute cycles with a break of five minutes for water and rest at least once per week is beneficial.

Many spas are currently providing the option of a Far Infrared Sauna that is said to produce a more deeply penetrating internal heat so that the body will produce sweat. This is accomplished at a lower temperature of 120-150 degrees Fahrenheit, which makes it more tolerable for a longer period of time. Therefore, a duration of fifteen minutes, with a gradual increase of up to sixty minutes, can be safely added into your detoxification plan. Portable sauna units are also available for purchase at online stores for at-home use. Remember, regardless of which type of sweating treatment you use, it is important to hydrate well before, during, and after the experience and replenish lost electrolytes as a wellness precaution.

Epsom Salt Baths—Adding this mineral-rich compound to a hot bath serves a twofold purpose of giving the body much-needed minerals that are penetrated through the open pores of the skin, in addition to magnesium and sulfate, which helps the body to eliminate toxins via the skin. This therapeutic event can be enhanced with baking soda to neutralize chlorine in your unfiltered bath water and essential oils to stimulate aroma filled relaxation.

Directions:

Bathtub full of hot water

2 cups of Epsom salt

1 cup of baking soda

7-10 drops of an essential oil of your choice (lavender helps with relaxation).

Contrast Shower—This hydrotherapy technique manipulates the power of hot and cold water to strengthen your immune system, and improves blood circulation that helps the body to more readily release toxins.

Directions:

Complete 3 full cycles of hot and cold showering. Always begin with hot and end with cold; the greater the contrast between hot and cold temperatures, the greater the benefits.

One cycle includes:

3 minutes of hot showering

1 minute of cold showering

Do a total of three cycles; you can begin with more comfortable temperatures and continue to adjust accordingly to build up a tolerance of greater contrast.

Dry Skin Brushing—Prior to getting in your contrast shower start your detoxification process by obtaining a natural loofah brush to practice this therapy of exfoliating dead skin and improving the circulation of blood and lymphatic drainage.

Directions:

Always brush skin toward the heart

Begin with toes and work upward

From fingertips inward toward the chest

From neck downward toward the heart (do not brush your face)

Repeat this process for 5-10 minutes

Conclude with a (contrast) shower

OTHER DETOX THERAPIES

Castor Oil Pack—This time-tested oil has a variety of medicinal benefits with detoxification of the lymphatic channels when applied topically. For widest coverage apply over the liver (found on right side of upper abdominal area).

Directions:

For best absorption choose flannel material that can be folded into a 3-layer pack

Saturate flannel in castor oil so that it is penetrated through all layers

Apply saturated flannel over the liver

Hold flannel securely in place and use plastic wrap to bind pack to abdomen

Wipe off any excess oil

Open a plastic garbage bag to lay on to ensure you will not mess up your sheets (*castor oil stains so be careful*)

Lay on bag with face up

Apply towel over abdomen and place a heating pad over area for 15 minutes

After 15 minutes remove heating pad

Continue with castor oil pack only for an additional 45 minutes or overnight

Upon removing castor oil pack use baking soda and warm water to remove oil from body

Used packs can be placed in a resealable plastic bag and stored in the refrigerator, so that oils will not become rancid. Continue to use until pack changes colors or begins to smell bad from oxidization.

Massage Therapy—Any time is a great time for the art of touching, especially while detoxing because it enhances the overall benefits of a detox by aiding in the body's ability to relax, increase the circulation, break-up adhesion in fascia and muscle tissue, and release pent-up emotions that can be trapped in the tissue as well. 30-60 minutes or longer full-body massages are recommended at least 1-4 times per month. Also, obtaining a 10-15 minute abdominal massage immediately before or during colon hydrotherapy stimulates the colon and increases the release of fecal matter.

Complaint Fast—This is another way to support your spiritual and mental/emotional vitality. For a given number of days you make an intentional choice not to complain about anything. We live in a society where complaining is the norm; we build communities of people who share our same complaints, whether it is in our neighborhood or in the checkout line at the supermarket. Many of our conversations with strangers begin as we complain that the cashier line is not moving fast enough, this store is always out of our favorite product, and so forth. We complain about the driver in front of us being in a greater rush to get to work than we are. We complain about the evening news anchor's lipstick being the wrong shade for her complexion or his tie being too colorful for TV. It does not take much for us to find something to complain about or be pulled into a conversation of someone else's complaints. As you are consciously choosing to not complain what is being brought to your awareness is just how much people complain about every big or small thing. You will also notice just how easy it is to agree with them and begin to vent your own frustrations about your long list of complaints regarding your spouse, job, children, parents, neighborhood, politics, government, economy, church, media, etc. Once you are aware of just how much you complain throughout the week, you will also notice that eliminating complaints from your daily verbal exercises is more than a notion because complaints for many are more second nature than gratitude. But like all things, this bad habit can be changed with practice.

Complaints are from a negative place and gratitude is from a positive place. When we slow down enough to choose not to complain, it opens the doorway for compassion and decreases the immediate impulse to believe that whatever we are complaining about was somehow a personal attack on us. Your neighbor across the street who did not cut his or her hedges on the same weekend you cut yours to keep the block looking unified may have experienced a family emergency that distracted his or her time, energy, and attention away from insignificant things like landscaping. The driver on the road weaving in and out of traffic may have received her final warning for being tardy to work, with the next incident resulting in termination, therefore her driving patterns have nothing to do with you. If it is not causing you any danger on the road, it really isn't impacting your life at all, so the point in complaining would be what?

Meditation as discussed earlier helps with the art of practicing "mindfulness" when cruising through life. We become better positioned to being slow to judge and quick to just allow life to be, putting more effort into finding the good in ourselves, in others, and in the world in which we live: those are some of the benefits of this no complaints fast. This can be done for ten days or longer. For most optimal benefits do it for twenty-one consistent days, meaning that whenever you mess up you must start back at Day 1 again. You are creating a new habit so it may take a few times just to become more mindful of how much you do complain and then work to change that into something positive.

Counseling—While you are embarking on the journey to clean out all the toxic waste particles from your body, this would be a good time to begin some talk therapy sessions with a professional counselor to help you cleanse your mental and emotional selves. Unlike some of the other supplemental therapies listed above, counseling for many will be an ongoing process over a specified or open-ended period of time. The benefits are more cumulative as you sit with a trained professional to work through any unresolved issues of self-worth, self-image, self-esteem, anger, betrayal, forgiveness, jealously, envy, hate, fear, rejection, trauma, neglect, abandonment, sadness, unhappiness, grief, and more. At some point throughout life, everyone will encounter any one or several of these feelings or incidents, however there is that segment of the population that will hold on to these life-taking feelings to the point that they become toxic inside the body. As I have reiterated in the forgiveness section, a toxic mind will over time have physical manifestations within the body that later develop into disease.

Here is an example from my work with a patient I once co-managed with another physician. The patient was interested in improved health and seeking out natural alternatives to current symptoms such as her lack of focus, poor memory, and difficulty sleeping. The twenty-four-year-old patient had been dealing with the sleeping difficulties for approximately two years and poor memory and lack of focus for one and a half years, which the latter prompted her to go to a doctor who then prescribed her Adderall—a typical pharmaceutical given for patients with attention deficit disorders (ADD). But she felt the drug was not helping her much.

In an attempt to get at the root of the problem, I asked her if she had ever experienced any trauma in her life, and her response was yes. As we talked more, her sleep difficulties occurred immediately following her traumatic event. At which time she began to take an over-the-counter (OTC) liquid sleeping aid that she was still taking at the time of our appointment to self-medicate her post-traumatic stress disorder (PTSD). She had never been to counseling to talk through her traumatic event and scars of unresolved fears that continued to linger long after the event had passed. Her mental and emotional upset inhibited her ability to relax enough at night to go to sleep (a natural process) without help. The methods she was using to put her to sleep were only getting her to a Level 2 stage of sleep (there are four stages that the body cycles through all throughout the duration of sleep). She was not reaching the essential third and fourth stages of sleep for almost two years, which means that her body was resting every night but not being restored on a cellular level; this would naturally cause some neurological difficulties in memory and focus. One of the best things you can do for your memory is give it a good quality, deep sleep. With the combination of her extremely poor dietary habits, she wasn't giving her body the basic essentials to thrive and it showed.

As a naturopathic doctor, I am trained to always look at the root cause first and work my way upward and outward toward the surface manifestations. This patient example, among so many others, demonstrates that her symptoms of poor memory and focus that motivated her initial visit to the first doctor were not indicative that the body was communicating a lack of a foreign substance known as Adderall. It was clear to me that the patient definitely needed to begin experiencing a restorative sleep and supplementation would be involved to support the body's built-in relaxation pathways. However, the end-goal for me was not to simply substitute her sleeping aid with a natural one but to ultimately remove the barriers that were inhibiting her ability to relax. For me, this would be difficult to achieve without the patient receiving therapeutic counseling to deal with her PTSD.

Applying these other supportive therapies to your lifestyle or periods of detoxification will help in your journey of holistically keeping your entire being cleansed. There is power is the synergistic effect of toxic removal that will keep you on the path toward optimized health and wellness.

CHAPTER 14

DETOX-STYLE

PILLARS OF A DETOX-STYLE

1. **IDENTIFY** your daily controllable toxic exposures

2. **LIMIT** your daily exposures to toxins as much as possible

3. **SUPPORT** your detoxification pathways daily through diet, movement, water, and self-expression

4. **CLEANSE** your whole health with supportive therapies at regular intervals.

IN THE EARLIER CHAPTERS OF THIS BOOK I IDENTIFIED HOW MULTIPLE toxic exposures are constant throughout each and every day. Becoming intentional about limiting those daily exposures as much as possible reduces the impact that toxins can have on accelerating the deterioration of the body. Through ongoing daily support of detoxification pathways via diet, exercise, water, and self-expressing the life you are here to live, you can prevent blockages and stagnation. This will help toxins freely move out of the body without obstructions. Lastly, cleansing your whole health with supportive therapies and implementing more intensive detoxification practices at regular intervals throughout the year gives the body all the necessary resources it needs to self-recover, rejuvenate, and restore itself through a Detox-style. Living a Detox-style equips you with tools to ultimately enhance your life by taking your health to the next level of wholeness.

As you adopt a Detox-style of living, I want to re-emphasize how the foods we eat impact the level of detoxing our bodies will do. On the following pages are charts that illustrate a few examples of levels that you may choose to live out your Detox-style of eating, with term highlights and brief explanations on how to use the charts found on pages 122–124. Each chart has five rows beginning with the top row indicating the level of detox results (row 1) based off of the type of meals you consume (row 2), whether or not the ingredients in the meals are organic vs. conventional (row 3), whether or not the foods you consume are raw or cooked (row 4) and lastly, how many meals/smoothies you consume per day (row 5).

MEAL IMPACT ON DETOX

RESULTS	OPTIMAL ⟷ MODERATE ⟷ NONE				
	Raw Juices & Liquids	Green Smoothies	Vegan Vegetarian	Meat & Vegetables (no processed foods)	Meat with packaged & processed foods
Type of Meals					
Organic (O) or conventional (C) ingredients	100% organic	80% (O) 20% (C)	50% (O) 50% (C)	20% (O) 80% (C)	100% conventional
Raw or cooked	100% raw	80% raw 20% cooked	50% raw 50% cooked	20% raw 80% cooked	100% cooked
Meals per day & type	Juices and liquids only	Green smoothies only	1 meal & green smoothies	2 meals and green smoothie	3 meals or more

FASTING ONLY

RESULTS	OPTIMAL	MODERATE			NONE
Type of Meals	Raw Juices & Liquids	Green Smoothies	Vegan Vegetarian	Meat & Vegetables (no processed foods)	Meat with packaged & processed foods
Organic (O) or conventional (C) ingredients	100% organic	80% (O) 20% (C)	50% (O) 50% (C)	20% (O) 80% (C)	100% conventional
Raw or cooked	100% raw	80% raw 20% cooked	50% raw 50% cooked	20% raw 80% cooked	100% cooked
Meals per day & type	Juices and liquids only	Green smoothies only	1 meal & green smoothies	2 meals and green smoothie	3 meals or more

HIGH LEVEL OF MODERATE EATING

RESULTS	OPTIMAL ——→		MODERATE ——→			NONE
Type of Meals	Raw Juices & Liquids	Green Smoothies	Vegan	Vegetarian	Meat & Vegetables (no processed foods)	Meat with packaged & processed foods
Organic (O) or conventional (C) ingredients	100% organic	80% (O) 20% (C)	50% (O) 50% (C)		20% (O) 80% (C)	100% conventional
Raw or cooked	100% raw	80% raw 20% cooked	50% raw 50% cooked		20% raw 80% cooked	100% cooked
Meals per day & type	Juices and liquids only	Green smoothies only	1 meal & green smoothies		2 meals and green smoothie	3 meals or more

LOW LEVEL OF MODERATE EATING

RESULTS	OPTIMAL ←	→ MODERATE ←		→ NONE
Type of Meals	Raw Juices & Liquids	Green Smoothies	Vegan Vegetarian	Meat & Vegetables (no processed foods)	Meat with packaged & processed foods
Organic (O) or conventional (C) ingredients	100% organic	80% (O) 20% (C)	50% (O) 50% (C)	20% (O) 80% (C)	100% conventional
Raw or cooked	100% raw	80% raw 20% cooked	50% raw 50% cooked	20% raw 80% cooked	100% cooked
Meals per day & type	Juices and liquids only	Green smoothies only	1 meal & green smoothies	2 meals and green smoothie	3 meals or more

STANDARD LEVEL

RESULTS	OPTIMAL ⟵	⟶ MODERATE ⟵	⟶		NONE
Type of Meals	Raw Juices & Liquids	Green Smoothies	Vegan Vegetarian	Meat & Vegetables (no processed foods)	Meat with packaged & processed foods
Organic (O) or conventional (C) ingredients	100% organic	80% (O) 20% (C)	50% (O) 50% (C)	20% (O) 80% (C)	100% conventional
Raw or cooked	100% raw	80% raw 20% cooked	50% raw 50% cooked	20% raw 80% cooked	100% cooked
Meals per day & type	Juices and liquids only	Green smoothies only	1 meal & green smoothies	2 meals and green smoothie	3 meals or more

DISEASE LEVEL

RESULTS	OPTIMAL ←→		MODERATE ←→		NONE
Type of Meals	Raw Juices & Liquids	Green Smoothies	Vegan Vegetarian	Meat & Vegetables (no processed foods)	Meat with packaged & processed foods
Organic (O) or conventional (C) ingredients	100% organic	80% (O) 20% (C)	50% (O) 50% (C)	20% (O) 80% (C)	100% conventional
Raw or cooked	100% raw	80% raw 20% cooked	50% raw 50% cooked	20% raw 80% cooked	100% cooked
Meals per day & type	Juices and liquids only	Green smoothies only	1 meal & green smoothies	2 meals and green smoothie	3 meals or more

HOW TO USE THE MEAL IMPACT ON DETOX CHARTS

TERM HIGHLIGHTS

Raw & living foods—Raw and living foods are those foods eaten in their natural whole state such as fruits, vegetables, nuts, seeds, and sprouts. These foods can be soaked and sprouted to ease digestion as well as dehydrated to alter texture without destroying important digestive enzymes. The destruction of these vital enzymes happens whenever foods are heated beyond 116 degrees Fahrenheit.

Raw juices—100% pure fresh-squeezed or fresh-pressed vegetable, fruit, or combination juices that do not include any other ingredients and are NOT made from concentrate.

Liquids only—Can include raw juices, natural liquid mixtures such as (lemonade mixture—see Chapter 15) or vegetable broths.

Green Smoothies—Blended beverages that includes a liquid base, dark leafy greens, other vegetables, fruits optional, and plant-based protein powder is optional.

Organic foods—Foods that have not been produced in synthetic fertilizers, they do not contain any pesticides, hormones, antibiotics, growth regulators, artificial ingredients, or genetically modified organisms (GMOs).

Conventional Foods— (non-organic) those foods that may contain GMOs, artificial ingredients, hormones, antibiotics, growth regulators, pesticides, and produced in synthetic fertilizer.

Vegan Meals—Consuming plant based foods (i.e. fruits, vegetables, nuts, seeds, legumes, and grains) that do not contain any meat, poultry, or seafood ingredients or their by-products.

Vegetarian Meals—Excludes meat and poultry from dietary habits while continuing to consume animal by-products and/or seafood. Some sub-set vegetarian lifestyle labels can include:

Lacto-ovo vegetarian—vegetarians who consume dairy (i.e. cheese, milk, and yogurt) and eggs.

Ovo-vegetarian—vegetarians who consume eggs and no dairy.

Pescetarian or Pesco-vegetarian—vegetarians who consume seafood products with or without intake of dairy and eggs.

Processed & Packaged Foods—This includes meals and food items that have been pre-made, boxed or canned, frozen, or packaged meals to make it easy for you to "heat & eat," "just add water & eat," or "pour & eat." Snack foods such as cookies, cakes, chips, crackers, and boxed cereals are also common purchases in this category.

MEAL CHART TYPES

Fasting-Only Chart—The most optimal results as mentioned in Chapter 11 will always be fasting on raw juices and liquids. This level should ONLY be used for monthly, quarterly, semi-annual, or annual intervals only for a very specific amount of time (see list below) in conjunction with other supportive therapies to ensure bowel elimination.

High/Moderate Level Chart—Consuming primarily organic, eating more raw foods per day such as green smoothies, other raw meals that include salads, fresh fruit, nuts and seeds, and one cooked vegan meal per day.

Low/Moderate Level Chart—Consuming meats (organic, grass-fed, wild-caught) with other organic primarily organic fresh and/or cooked vegetables, fruit, nuts, seeds, and minimal carbohydrates. No packaged or processed foods are included.

Standard Level Chart—Consuming meat with processed and packaged foods made with at least 20% organic ingredients and at least 20% raw foods. This level involves eating three or more meals per day.

Disease Level Chart—To ensure some level of detox benefits from daily food consumption, avoid each eating food based on each of these characteristics all in the same day. For each characteristic you choose from this column, balance it out by choosing a characteristic from one of the more impactful columns. Such as if you are eating all of your meals cooked, choose 80% or more organic ingredients and make

1 or more of the meals are vegan to limit your toxic exposure.

To further enhance your new Detox-style beyond eating is a suggested list of how to regularly combine the various supportive therapies mentioned throughout this book to continuously revitalize your health.

DAILY CLEANSE TIPS

- Food (Eating less from the avoid list and more from the consume list) also refer to Meal Impact Charts on pages 116–121.

- Movement (Includes: Aerobic Exercise/Strength Training/Yoga/Stretching)

- Water

- Sleep

- Bowel Movements

- Gratitude Journal

- Meditation/Prayer

- Self-Expression

WEEKLY CLEANSE TIPS

- Epsom salt baths

- Sauna

- Dry skin brushing

- Contrast Shower

- Vaginal Steam (Females Only)

- Thought process journaling

- Counseling (weekly/biweekly)

MONTHLY CLEANSE TIPS

- Massage

- Castor Oil Pack

- 3-day fast (Friday 6PM – Monday 6AM) – Combined with an enema

- 3-day "no complaints" fast

- Creative arts activity

- Working through forgiveness (new or reoccurring encounters)

QUARTERLY CLEANSE TIPS

- 10-day detox (Level 2 or 3—see Chapter 15), combined with enemas and/or herbal supplementation

- Colon Hydrotherapy (Colonic)

SEMIANNUAL/ANNUAL CLEANSE TIPS

- 21-30 days Detox (Levels 1, 2, & 3—see Chapter 15) combined with herbal supplementation

- 21 days "no complaints" fast

- Re-evaluation of relationships

- Mental/emotional wellness check-up with a licensed therapist

- Comprehensive wellness check-up with a naturopathic physician

CHAPTER 15

DETOXIFICATION PROTOCOLS

DETOX LEVELS

> Level 1—Elimination Diet
>
> Level 2—Elimination Diet & Smoothies
>
> Level 3—Smoothies & Fluids Only

DETOX LEVEL OPTIONS

1. Choose one detox level you would like to do for at least 10 days (1, 2, or 3)

2. Choose Levels 1 & 2 or 2 & 3 detox protocols to do for a full 20 days (10 days at each level)

3. Choose Levels 1, 2 & 3 detox protocols to do for a full 30 days (10 days at each level) Beginning with Level 1 and working your way up to Level 3.

BELOW IS A DETAILED LAYOUT OF EACH LEVEL. FOR THE PERSON BRAND new to detoxification and fasting, starting out at Level 1 with an Elimination Diet is recommended as you adjust your body to eating a simple yet healthy diet that will help it cleanse. Staying consistent and committed throughout the length of time you have selected to detox is more important than starting out at a high level and only successfully completing one to two days.

LEVEL 1: ELIMINATION DIET

This level consists of eating small, frequent meals throughout the day that includes breakfast, lunch, and dinner, with one to two optional snacks. You should not eat to the point of feeling stuffed but to the point of satisfaction. Only foods on the consumption list should be consumed, and all foods on the avoid list should be eliminated from your diet during this time of cleansing. Please refer to charts in Chapter 14 as a guide in determining the foods you will eat during the detox. Suggested menu options, smoothie preparation tips, and complete meal salads are listed at the end of this section.

FOOD CONSUMPTION LIST:

Vegetables: Fresh organic vegetables of your choice can include arugula, artichokes, asparagus, beets, bell peppers, broccoli, Brussels sprouts, cabbage, carrots, cauliflower, celery, collards, cucumbers, dandelion, eggplants, kale, lettuce, mushrooms, parsnips, pumpkin, radishes, rutabagas, spinach, sweet potatoes, Swiss chard, turnips, and yams. Sea vegetables such as arame, dulse, hiziki, kombu, and nori.

Herbs: basil, cilantro, fennel, garlic, ginger, onion, parsley, tumeric

Fruits: apples, avocado, blackberries, blueberries, cherries, lemons, limes, oranges pears, pomegranates, raspberries, strawberries, and tomatoes.

Nuts and Seeds (raw and unsalted): almonds, brazil nuts, cashews, hazelnuts, pecans, and walnuts. Seeds include chia, flax, hemp, pumpkin, sesame, and sunflower seeds. Nuts and seeds have a high fat content; therefore, consume in moderation (max of 1-2 servings per day—nuts 1/4 cup; seeds 1-2 tbsps.).

Whole Grains: whole grain oats, quinoa, wild rice, or brown rice (limit to 2 servings of ½ cups cooked per day)

Legumes (dried beans): navy, white, black, mung, lima, butter, black-eyed peas, broad (fava), garbanzo (chickpeas), pinto, lentils, and split peas, and fermented soy beans.

AVOID FOODS:

All refined grains: any foods made with white flour, white pasta, and white rice, other white or instant cook grains (i.e., grits, rice, and oats)

All animal-based dairy products: milk, cheese, ice cream, butter, yogurt, and kiefer

Eggs

All meats: beef, pork, chicken, turkey, seafood, veal, and lamb

All fried foods

All fast food

All processed and packaged foods: chips, crackers, snack foods, boxed cereals, frozen meals, canned foods, pre-made shelved meals

All alcohol: beer, wine, liquor

All sweeteners: white sugar, brown sugar, honey, agave nectar, (*maple syrup ingredient in the lemonade detox drink is acceptable*)

All desserts and baked goods: cookies, cakes, candies, pies, rolls, and all breads

All sodas and juices (except for natural fresh pressed juices for fasting purposes)

All caffeine (coffee, tea, energy drinks)

LEVEL 1 SAMPLE MENU OPTIONS

For specific recipes for any of the items listed below refer to any Raw/Living Foods Prep books, Vegan Cookbooks, or online shared recipe sites.

Suggested Breakfast Options:

Green vegetable & fruit smoothie

2-3 servings of 1 fruit (apples, berries, oranges, etc.)

1 bowl of mixed raw fruit sprinkled with ground flaxseed

Raw chopped fruit with dairy-free yogurt

Whole grain oatmeal topped with berries and cinnamon

½ cup of natural granola & plant based milk (almond, oat, rice, or coconut)

Chia seed pudding topped with fresh berries

Suggested Lunch and Dinner Options:

Mixed greens salad with light vinaigrette dressing topped with raw vegetables (i.e., beets, carrots, cucumbers, chives, mushrooms, olives, onions, etc.), and your choice of beans. With ¼ baked sweet potato

Steamed vegetables (i.e. carrots, broccoli, cauliflower, onions, garlic, and bell peppers) and black beans over brown rice

A small salad and quinoa with soup

Black bean soup

Split-pea soup

Vegetable soup

Lentil soup

Collard green wrap of hummus and vegetables of choice (i.e.

shredded carrots, bell peppers, and sprouts)

SUGGESTED SNACKS (OPTIONAL)

Apple with 2 tbsp. of peanut butter

Cucumber with diced tomatoes

¼ cup of raw nuts

Celery sticks or broccoli with hummus

2 tbsp. of guacamole with bell pepper sticks

½ cup of granola with or without milk

Green smoothie blending options, yields 20 oz.

Choose 1 base, 1 dark leafy green, 2-3 vegetables, 1-2 fruits, 1-2 additives

BASE	VEGETABLES/ HERBS	FRUITS (OPTIONAL)	ADDITIVES
10 oz. base Spring Water Non-dairy Milk (Almond, Coconut, Oat or Rice) OR 5oz. of pure (not from concentrate) apple juice diluted with 5oz. of water OR *5 oz. of pure Tomato juice diluted in 5 oz. of water (for vegetable smoothies)	1 handful of greens; Dark leafy greens (kale, spinach, Swiss chard, spring mix, dandelion); 1 small handful of 2-3 items: Carrots/ Celery/ Broccoli/ Cauliflower/ Cucumber/ Sprouts/ Bell peppers/ Parsley Basil/ Cilantro (for vegetable only smoothies)/ Ginger (1 tsp)/ Garlic (1 clove for vegetable only smoothies)	½ cup (max) mix 1-2 fruits Blueberries Strawberries Raspberries Blackberries Avocado Tomato ½ Apple ¼ Lemon (with peel) ¼ Ripe Banana	1 ½ tbsp. seeds Flax seeds Chia seeds Hemp seeds Plant-based Protein powder (1-2 scoops)

BLENDING TIPS

For a THICKER smoothie use LESS fluid base or more ice and for a THINNER smoothie use MORE fluid base and less or no ice.

Create combinations of flavors based on suggestions above and your personal taste buds or be adventurous and explore other natural ingredients to include that are not listed.

For vegetable only smoothies, adding a pinch of sea salt and/or cayenne pepper is optional to enhance flavor.

The quality of the smoothie will depend on how powerful your blender is. Low quality blenders will usually not blend all ingredients into a very smooth beverage. Chop up veggies and fruits into finer pieces to create a smoother consistency. Consider investing in a commercial-quality blender such as a Vitamix or Blendtec once you experience yourself using a blender several times per week consistently over a two-to-three-month period and you have burned out at least one blender (this means you are blending regularly and are now ready for an upgrade).

DETOX SMOOTHIE

2-5 oz. of pure apple juice

5-8 oz. of filtered water (liquid base should equal 10 oz.)

¾ cup of frozen mixed berries

1 generous handful of mixed greens

3 stems of parsley

2- ½ in. thick cucumber slices (chopped)

1 celery stalk

¼ of lemon with peel

½ tsp of fresh cut ginger

2 tbsp. of ground flax seeds

Blend for 45 seconds or until smooth

SALAD INGREDIENTS OPTIONS

Begin with 1 bed of greens (2 cups); 2-3 vegetables; 1-2 herb; 1-2 proteins; 1 toppings (1 tbsp.); 2 tbsp. of oil-based dressing; non-oil dressing such as lemon juice or vinegar can be used more generously.

GREENS	VEGGIES	HERBS	PLANT PROTEINS	OTHER
Arugula Cabbage Dandelion Kale Mixed Greens Spinach Swiss chard	Artichoke hearts Avocado Beets Bell Pepper Broccoli Brussel Sprouts Carrots Celery Cucumber Fennel Mushrooms Olives Peas Radish Snap Peas Sprouts Sun-dried tomato Sprouts Tomatoes	Basil Cilantro Chives Dill Onions Oregano Parsley Pepper Red Pepper Flakes Thyme	Beans Chickpeas Hummus Tempeh	Quinoa Raw nuts/- seeds (i.e. almonds, walnuts, cashews, sunflower seeds, flax seeds, chia seeds)

COMPLETE MEAL SALAD

1 bed of mixed greens

1 small handful of sprouts

Shredded carrots

Sliced cucumbers

Chives

Diced tomatoes

½ cup of black beans

¼ of an avocado (cubed)

2 tbsp. of salad dressing (see recipe below)

LITE VINAIGRETTE SALAD DRESSING

ACID	OIL	FLAVOR	SEASONING
Lemon Juice Lime Juice Vinegar	Fresh Pressed Extra Virgin Olive Oil	Minced Garlic Minced Onions	Sea salt Nutritional Yeast

SALAD DRESSING YIELDS 4 TBSP. (2 SERVINGS OF 2 TBSP.)

4 tbsp. of lemon juice

1 tbsp. of olive oil

1 pinch of salt

1 clove of minced garlic

2 tbsp. of nutritional yeast

LEVEL 2 ELIMINATION DIET & GREEN SMOOTHIES

This level includes slowly transitioning to green smoothies as a meal replacement of all solid foods. Refer to Level 1 Food Consumption List and Suggested Menu.

Days 1–2

Breakfast: Green Smoothie

Lunch, Dinner, & Snacks: Elimination Diet - Refer to Level 1 Food Consumption List and Menu

Days 3–4

Breakfast & Lunch: Green Smoothie

Dinner & Snacks: Elimination Diet

Days 5–6

One Elimination Diet Meal per day (your choice of breakfast, lunch, dinner, or snacks)

Green Smoothies for the remainder of the day

Days 7–10

Green Smoothies ONLY all day

LEVEL 3: SMOOTHIES & FASTING

This level includes slowly transitioning off green smoothies to a diet inclusive of thin liquids only. These liquids can include: water, fresh pressed natural juices (vegetable, vegetable fruit combinations, and fruit juice in moderation) lemonade diet mixture, and vegetable broth. If you do not have your own juicer or live near a juice bar, you can prepare your own fresh lemonade detox mixture at home as a stand-alone liquid option for a fresh nutritional beverage that will sustain you during your fast.

LEMONADE DETOX MIXTURE

Items needed for 1 gallon:

Gallon size container

Gallon of filtered water

8 organic whole lemons

14 ozs. organic Grade B maple syrup

1 ½ tsp. organic cayenne pepper

Directions:

Wash lemons and squeeze juice from each one into a small bowl; filter out all seeds

In a gallon sized container pour in 8 cups of filtered water followed by 14 ozs. of organic Grade B maple syrup, next pour in all the lemon juice, add 1 ½ tsp. of organic cayenne pepper, then add remaining water up to 1 gallon mark. Shake vigorously. Drink 8 cups per day in addition to water.

3 gallons will accommodate Level 3 Protocol drink 8 cups per day on fasting only days and up to 2 cups per meal on days when green smoothies are consumed.

Days 1–2

Green Smoothies ONLY all day

Days 3–4

One meal of liquids ONLY

Green Smoothies for remainder of the day

Days 5–6

Smoothies for one meal

Liquids ONLY for remainder of the day

Days 7–10

Liquids ONLY all day

When completing Level 2 as a stand-alone detox or upon completion of Level 3 please follow these instructions carefully

SOLID FOOD TRANSITION

Keep portion sizes small to slowly awaken the digestive tract and reduce any abdominal discomfort.

Day 11

Breakfast: Fresh raw juicy fruit (i.e. orange, apple, pear, pineapple)

Lunch & Dinner: Small Salad topped with a medley of vegetables and a cup of vegetable soup

Day 12

Breakfast: Fresh raw juicy fruit (i.e. orange, apple, pear, pineapple)

Lunch: Small Salad topped with a medley of vegetables and a cup of vegetable soup

Dinner: Salad or steamed vegetables with brown rice

CONCLUSION

WE HAVE BEEN GIVEN A BODY THAT IS BUILT TO THRIVE AT ALL costs; it is strong, it is resilient, and it is powerful. That is when it has all the necessary resources to operate at optimal capacity. Although the body was created to self-heal and self-repair throughout each and every day, living in a toxic filled environment impedes upon its ability to do so.

Throughout the pages of this book I have listed many of our most common toxic exposures not including the various radiation-emitting devices such as cell phones and personal computers. Nonetheless, all toxic exposures are contributing moment by moment to diminishing our health, which ultimately impacts our quality of life. For many of you, the long list of toxins outlined in this book may be downright overwhelming because, no matter what, there is no way to live and not be exposed to them in the modern world. As important as it is to be fully aware of what the toxic exposures are, the epicenter is in knowing how do we coexist with these toxins, and that power lies in the hands of each and every individual. We have the power to speed up the toxic exposures and the diminishment of our health or slow down our exposures and minimize their adverse health effects through adopting a holistic Detox-style that will provide ongoing support to our health and well-being.

You now have the designation of being not only an informed consumer but also someone who is proactive about your health. If this were not true, you would not have picked up this book. With your new designation you get to exercise your power of choice with both knowledge and wisdom. The facts have been provided about daily toxic exposures, along with daily practices to make it a lifestyle change that you can participate in that will holistically support and tonify your life from the inside outward.

Choose holistic continually, each and every time. When you are connecting with your divine energy source, fully expressing what you are here to do, joyful about life, at peace with yourself, and satisfied in your loving relationships, there is nothing limiting your mind and spirit to break through every barrier, every negative condition, every obstacle to keep your physical body intact to thrive. Just as toxins attack the physical body and must be released, a Detox-style of keeping our spiritual, mental, emotional selves cleansed are equally as important to live the optimal life that is our divine birthright.

"(S)He who has health has hope and (s)he who has hope has everything."
—Arabian Proverb

AFTERWORD

W E LIVE IN A SOCIETY WHOSE HEALTH CARE INFRASTRUCTURE IS dictated primarily by profit-driven insurance companies and pharmaceutical drug companies. You do not have to play the role of innocent bystander anymore and participate in a system that at first glance is set up to work for you, but behind the scenes is questionable. Throughout these pages I have talked a lot about licensed naturopathic physicians and the holistic natural approach that we take in understanding the root cause of your health disturbances. We provide individualized wellness plans to help you optimize your health and wellness, thereby optimizing your quality of life. If you have not visited a licensed naturopath in the past, it is my recommendation that you do for the sake of being informed and empowered in disease prevention or managing your disease from the level of root causes with natural complementary therapies.

I have emphasized "licensed" naturopaths because in many states there is no legislation in place to inform the consumer of those doctors who have attended an accredited four-year residential medical school, and who have completed clinical training and national board exams to equip them to safely diagnose and manage diseased conditions in the body. Without this legislation in place to license naturopaths, consumers are not protected from the multitude of "herbalists" who identify themselves as "naturopathic doctors." Unbekownst to patients these herbalists, while providing great value to the natural health community, are not academically and clinically trained to safely provide disease diagnosis and treatment. Nonetheless, the greatest downside of naturopathic licensing laws not being in place is that you as the consumer have no way of knowing who you are entrusting your medical care to, if you don't ask outright. Another significant component to many states currently not providing licensure is that it restricts the option of health insurance coverage for the services we provide.

Unfortunately for you as the patient, naturopathic doctors practicing in unlicensed states do not accept insurance and those that are practicing in licensed states usually don't either because it significantly reduces the time they are allowed to spend with patients to get to the "root cause." However, in those licensed states many patients, (depending on your insurance company) can file a claim for reimbursement. Therefore, when states don't provide a scope of practice for licensure, these legislative limitations restrict the option of insurance reimbursements even being available for patients of naturopathic doctors. For more information on how to get involved with legislation so that board-certified naturopathic doctors can become licensed in your state to increase the option of insurance reimbursements please visit *www.naturopathic.org* and click on the advocacy tab.

Nevertheless, the bottom line is, unless you have a Health Savings Account (HSA) or Flexible Spending Account (FSA) card, which is accepted by naturopaths in all states, obtaining our services will more likely than not be an out-of-pocket expense. This should be viewed as a sound investment in your health. Oftentimes people find it challenging to get beyond the thought that if their insurance does not cover a wellness expense, then they cannot justify paying for it on their own. Keep in mind that insurance companies are businesses whose main priority is to make money, while they assist with your healthcare needs. The priority of preserving your health is your job and you should not intentionally give that type of power and control over to anyone while you have your own mental and physical faculties. As long as the things that insurance covers under your plans aligns with their mission to financially capitalize off of your disease (not wellness) then everyone benefits.

Inside the database of your insurance company you are not a person living the fullness of life and all that it means, you are a name with a case number and a list of health codes associated with it. Why leave the power in their hands about how much your health is worth to them? The real question is how much is your health worth to you? Spending the few hundred dollars to get a comprehensive health assessment annually and several supplements to support and tonify your organ systems that are out of balance is more than worth it to your body that is continuing to age and deteriorate every day. Spending your golden years having a strong quality of life by making the proper investment in your health today is a lot more beneficial to your well-being than building a schedule around frequent doctor visits, medications, and lab tests that your insurance company is helping you pay for. Who is reimbursing you for all the time lost maintaining a sick life versus the free time you will have living a healthy one?

"So many people spend their health gaining wealth, then have to spend their wealth gaining health."
—A. J. Reb Materi

NEXT STEPS

Sign up for FREE to receive online detoxification resources, recipes, monthly newsletters, and other educational materials to help you maintain your Detox-style. Register at
www.mydetoxstyle.com

REFERENCES

"Antibiotic use in Food Producing Animals." Available from http://www.cdc.gov/narms/animals.html

"Food Safety." Retrieved from http://www.who.int/foodsafety/areas_work/food-technology/faq-genetically-modified-food/en/

"GE Food and your Health." Retrieved from http://www.centerforfoodsafety.org/issues/311/ge-foods/ge-food-and-your-health

"Your kidneys and how they work." (May 2014) Retreived from http://www.niddk.nih.gov/health-information/health-topics/Anatomy/kidneys-how-they-work/Pages/anatomy.aspx

Additives. Retrieved from http://www.sustainabletable.org/385/additives

Air Pollution Facts. Retrieved from http://www.conserve-energy-future.com/various-air-pollution-facts.php

Aktar, W., Sengupta, D., and Chowdhury, A. "Impact of pesticides use in agriculture: their benefits and hazards." Interdiscip Toxicol. 2009 Mar; 2(1): 1–12.

Badger, E. (2014 April 14) Pollution is segregated too. Retrieved from https://www.washingtonpost.com/news/wonk/wp/2014/04/15/pollution-is-substantially-worse-in-minority-neighborhoods-across-the-u-s/

Bailey, D. (2011 July) Gasping for Air: Toxic Pollutants Continue to Make Millions Sick and Shorten Lives. {Fact Sheet} Retrieved from http://www.nrdc.org/health/files/airpollutionhealthimpacts.pdf

Benzoic and Sodium Benzoate. (12 April 2005) Retrieved from http://www.who.int/ipcs/publications/cicad/cicad26_rev_1.pdf

Breast Cancer Fund. "Chemical in Plastics." Retrieved from http://

www.breastcancerfund.org/clear-science/environmental-breast-cancer-links/plastics/?referrer=https://www.google.com/

Chemical Cuisine. Retrieved from http://www.cspinet.org/reports/chemcuisine.htm

Cochineal Extract (7 May 2012) Retrieved from http://www.befoodsmart.com/ingredients/cochineal-extract.php#sthash.TWhGneho.dpuf

Cole, L. & Foster, S. From the Ground Up: Environmental Racism and Rise of the Environmental Justice Movement. New York University Press. 2001. P. 167

Cory, T "Toxic Relationships." Retrieved from http://www.healthscopemag.com/health-scope/toxic-relationships/

Crinnon, W. "Sauna as a Valuable Clinical Tool for Cardiovascular, Autoimmune, Toxicant induced and other Chronic Health Problems" Alter Med Rev 2011;16(3): 215-225.

Embryonic & Fetal Development. (2016) Retrieved from http://envirn.org/pg/pages/view/1344/embryonic-and-fetal-development

Friedman, M (2005). Fundamentals of Naturopathic Endocrinology. Toronto, ON. CCNM Press.

Gaby, A. (2011). Nutritional Medicine, Concord, NH.

Godfrey, A., Saunders, P. (2010). Principles & Practices of Naturopathic Botanical Medicine Vol I: Botanical Medicine Monographs. Toronto Ontario. CCNM Press.

Grossman, E. (5 Mar 2015) "Chemical Exposure Linked to Billions in Health Care Costs." Retrieved from http://news.nationalgeographic.com/news/2015/03/150305-chemicals-endocrine-disruptors-diabetes-toxic-environment-ngfood/

Grotheer, P., Marshall, M. and Simonne, A. Sulfites: Separating Fact from Fiction1. Retrieved from http://edis.ifas.ufl.edu/fy731

145

Hamlin H., Harley K., Susiarjo M., and Akingbemi B. (2009, Jan. 19) Common Chemical Increases Risks of Boys Genital Deformity. {Research Article Synopsis}. Retrieved from http://www.environmentalhealthnews.org/ehs/newscience/phthalates-increase-hypospadias-risk

Harvard C.H. Chan School of Public Health. (Winter 2011) "Plastics: Danger where we least expect it." Retrieved from http://www.hsph.harvard.edu/news/magazine/winter10plastics/

Health Impacts of Fine Particles in Air (2013 Dec. 7). Retrieved from http://ephtracking.cdc.gov/showAirHIA.action

Hetchtman, L. (2012). Clinical Naturopathic Medicine. Elsevier, Australia. Churchhill Livingstone.

James, M (2013, Jan. 14) How to Avoid Phthalates (Even Though you can't Avoid Phthalates) {Blog post}. Retrieved from http://www.huffingtonpost.com/maia-james/phthalates-health_b_2464248.html

Juliann Schaeffer and Tim Jewell (3 Mar 2016). Diabetes and MSG: What you Need to Know. Retrieved from http://www.healthline.com/health/diabetes/msg-what-you-need-to-know#Outlook7

Kostich, M. and Lazorchak, J. "Risks to aquatic organisms posed by human pharmaceutical use." Retrieved from http://www.epa.gov/sites/production/files/2014-09/documents/risks_to_aquatic_organisms_posed_by_human_pharma_use.pdf

Lau K, McLean WG, Williams DP, Howard CV. "Synergistic interactions between commonly used food additives in a developmental neurotoxicity test." Toxicol Sci. 2006 Mar;90(1):178-87.

McKenna, M. (24 Oct 2014). Farm Antibiotic Use: Getting Worse Before It (Maybe) Gets Better. Retrieved from http://theplate.nationalgeographic.com/2014/10/24/farm-antibiotic-use-getting-worse-before-it-maybe-gets-better/

Murtaugh, P. Jobs with an Increased Risk of Occupational Disease. Retrieved from http://www.nolo.com/legal-encyclopedia/

jobs-with-increased-risk-occupational-disease.html

National Cancer Institute (10 Jun 2011). "Formaldehyde and Cancer Risk." Retrieved from http://www.cancer.gov/about-cancer/causes-prevention/risk/substances/formaldehyde/formaldehyde-fact-sheet

National Center for Health Statistics (2014). Retrieved from http://www.cdc.gov/nchs/fastats/deaths.htm

Nitrates and Nitrites. Available from http://www.epa.gov

Occupational Respiratory Disease. Retrieved from http://familydoctor.org/familydoctor/en/prevention-wellness/staying-healthy/occupational-health/occupational-respiratory-disease.html

Paula, E. (2014 February 20) The Most Common Food Preservatives. Retrieved from http://www.livestrong.com/article/288335-the-most-common-food-preservatives/

Phthalates and Bisphenol A. (2014, Feb.) {Fact Sheet} Available from http://www.birthdefects.org/environmental-birth-defects/

Public Health & Environment. Retrieved from http://www.who.int/gho/phe/en/

Schreiber, C., Meyn, L., Creinin, M., Barnhart, K., and Hillier, S. "Effects of Long-Term Use of Nonoxynol-9 on Vaginal Flora." Obstet Gynecol. 2006 Jan; 107(1): 136–143.

Skocaj, M., Filipic, M., Petkovic, J., and Novak, S. "Titanium dioxide in our everyday life; is it safe?" Radiol Oncol. 2011 Dec; 45(4): 227–247.

The Health Consequences of Smoking—50 Years of Progress: A Report of the Surgeon General. Retrieved from http://www.surgeongeneral.gov/library/reports/50-years-of-progress/fact-sheet.html

The Statistics Portal. "Global plastic production from 1950 to 2014 (in million metric tons)." Retrieved from http://www.statista.com/statistics/282732/global-production-of-plastics-since-1950/

The Statistics Portal. Retrieved from http://www.statista.com/statistics/183505/number-of-vehicles-in-the-united-states-since-1990/ealth#.VqqBASorLIU

Toxins. (2015, April 30). Retrieved from https://www.nlm.nih.gov/medlineplus/ency/article/002331.htm

U. S. Food and Drug Administration. "Nail Care Products." Retrieved from http://www.fda.gov/Cosmetics/ProductsIngredients/Products/ucm127068.htm

U. S. National Library of Medicine. "Phthalates." Retrieved from http://toxtown.nlm.nih.gov/text_version/chemicals.php?id=24

Vehicles, Air Pollution, and Human Health. Retrieved from http://www.ucsusa.org/clean-vehicles/vehicles-air-pollution-and-human-health#.V5tit7grLIU

Weil, A. (1 Oct 2012) Retrieved from http://www.drweil.com/drw/u/QAA401181/Is-Carrageenan-Safe.html

WHO Definition of Health. (1948, April 7) Retrieved from http://www.who.int/about/definition/en/print.html

Women to Women. "The Lymph System and your Health." Retrieved from https://www.womentowomen.com/detoxification/the-lymph-system-and-your-health-2/2/

ACKNOWLEDGEMENTS

FIRST AND FOREMOST I AM TRULY GRATEFUL TO GOD FOR BLESSING MY life so richly along my journey of great challenges and great triumphs like bringing this book from a thought to full manifestation. I could not have completed the process by myself. It took a team of other talented, creative and supportive individuals to make publishing this book a reality for me. Those wonderful people include but are not limited to: Thomas Hill for providing editorial direction and layout support, Carol Maple for your behind-the-scenes assistance. Natasha Jordan of Map-It Inc. for securing the book cover design. Last but certainly not least, Mark Holland for photography.

I have also been blessed with a community of family and friends who have loved, nurtured, expanded, and supported my soul's purpose of growth and development. Those among honorable mention are: my Grandmother Dea for being my ambassador of what it means to be loving and kind even in the moments where it is neither reciprocated nor appreciated. Thank you for raising me and sacrificing yourself so that I could have the tools and resources to create a better life for myself and those I love.

To my grandfather, whom I call "Daddy" (may you rest in peace). Thank you for being my first example of a man who loved me and never expected anything in return.

Thank you to my parents who joined together so that I could come forth into this physical life. Mom, thank you for your love and support. Also, thanks to you and Eric for allowing me the time and space I needed to create and rebuild.

My "Broham," Chris, for being such a loving and caring uncle/brother, I will always cherish our abundance of great childhood memories together.

To my Uncle Leroy, Uncle Sunny, and Aunt Hester, thank you for your heart of support of me and my dreams.

Thanks to my close friends: Natasha, Jenine, Rosalind, Sichana, and Cicely, for allowing me to bend your ears for countless hours, being a shoulder to lean on, and a drinking fountain for encouragement and support that I could gain strength & renewal from.

Thanks to my mentors Cheryl, Dr. Rembert, and Dr. Lou. Cheryl, I appreciate you for always believing in me and seeing the best of what I had to offer long before I saw it in myself. You saw early on the love I have for the "Beloved Community" and you have nurtured that within me for decades and beyond. Dr. Rembert, thank you for your sound voice of guidance and wisdom. Dr. Lou, thank you for your passion and dedication for educating the next generation of naturopathic physicians.

Thanks to Rev. Celeste and Rev. Reggie for your words of light, wisdom, and inspiration, and praying me into the power of "I AM." There is a long list of other beautiful people that are family, friends, and colleagues that have journeyed and continue to journey along with me through this unfoldment of life and I am eternally grateful for each and every one of you for touching my life in the many ways that you have.

ABOUT THE AUTHOR

D R. T. HOUSTON IS A LICENSED NATUROPATHIC PHYSICIAN AT JOUR-
ney of Wellness Natural Medicine Center where she specializes in
providing natural forms of disease management and prevention
services to her patients. She obtained her doctorate in naturopathic medicine from National University of Health Sciences; a master of divinity
degree with a concentration in pastoral care and counseling from Princ-
eton Theological Seminary; and a bachelor of arts degree in sociology
from Howard University. She is very passionate about the synergy of the
mind, body, and spirit and facilitating the healing process of them collectively when working with patients. Dr. Houston has also participated
in international medical service trips to Nicaragua and Haiti with orga-
nizations such as Natural Doctors International and Naturopaths without Borders. She has served as an expert guest panelist at various health
related events on topics that include nutrition and holistic wellness. She
has been a featured guest on local television shows such as *Atlanta Live*,
Good News Primetime, and *The Nikhol B. Jackson Show* in addition to
several local radio talk shows. In her free time, Dr. Houston enjoys listening to poetry and live music.

To book Dr. Houston for your next health fair, speaking engagement,
seminar, workshop, or conference, please send your request to admin@
drthouston.com.

INDEX

A

Acne 9, 47
Allergies 9, 10
Antibiotics 33, 33, 44, 36, 51, 52, 73, 91
Antioxidants 72
Arthritis xvi
Asthma 9
Atherosclerosis 10, 21
Attention Deficit Disorder (ADD) 112
Autoimmune Diseases
   Lupus xvi
   Multiple Sclerosis xvi

B

Bacteria xx, xxi, 31, 33, 41, 44, 51, 52, 70, 90
Benzoates 30
Bowel Movements xx, 70, 72, 89, 91, 106, 110
Bronchitis 22

C

Cancer xvi, 4, 5, 21, 27, 29, 32, 33, 41, 48, 54, 70
Carbon Monoxide 22
Carcinogens 31, 32, 44, 45, 51, 56
Centers for Disease Control and Prevention (CDC) 20
Chronic Diseases
   Diabetes xvi, 10, 27, 30, 32
   Heart Disease xvi, 4, 5, 27, 29, 30
   High Cholesterol xvi
   Hypertension xvi, 32
Colon xx, 70, 71, 88, 89, 90, 91, 94, 105, 106, 110
Colon Cleansing 88, 105, 106
Colonoscopies 4
Colorectal Cancer 70
Counseling 111
Cruciferous vegetables 72

D

Depression 9
Detoxification Pathways

Cleansing xix, 8, 84, 85, 86, 79, 106, 90, 111
Fasting , 81, 82, 82, 103
Meals 79
Detox-style
    detoxification pathways iii, xvi, xix, 6, 8, 69, 71, 75
Dialysis, Kidney 5
Diet iii, 7, 71, 79, 71, 72, 74, 79, 93, 102, 106, 102
Dieting
    Elimination Diets , 126, 127, 79, 81, 102
Dust 24

E

Emunctories 69
Endocrine System Disruptors
    Parabens 44, 46, 48
    Phthalates 44, 46, 47, 51, 56
Endocrine Systems 10
Enemas 106
Estrogen 33, 38, 44, 56, 73
Exercise , 71, 72, 93, 93

F

Fasting , 81, 82, 82, 103
Fertility 10, 11
Fibroids xvi
Foods
    Additives and Preservatives xix, 27, 28, 29, 30, 34, 36
    Genetically Modified Organisms(GMOs) , 27
    Growth Hormones 33
Formaldehyde 45, 47, 48
Fossil Fuels 21

G

Gases 24
Gastrointestinal (GI) System 70
Genetically Modified Organisms (GMOs) , 27
Gout xvi

H

Health Care 3, 82, 57, 85, 88, 90, 83, 93, 93
High-Fructose Corn Syrup (HFCS) 32
Hip Bath 106
Hormones xvi, 5, 11, 33, 36, 43, 71, 72, 73, 56, 73, 74
    Estrogen 33, 38, 44, 56, 73
    Progesterone 33, 73
    Testosterone 33

Hydration xx, 37, 71, 91, 106
Hydrotherapy 105, 106, 108, 110

I

Infants 21, 25
Infertility 29, 56
Intentionality xiii, 7
Intestines 70
Intrauterine Devices (IUDs) 74

K

Kidneys 69

L

Landfills 21
Lead xx, 3, 8, 22, 23, 24, 33, 38, 43, 56, 72, 75
Liver 40, 44, 71, 72, 90, 109
Lungs 71, 97
Lymphatic System 71

M

Mammograms 4
Medications
    Over the Counter 41
    Prescription Medication 41
Meditation 71, 76, 95
Menopause xvi, 74
Menses 73, 74, 107
Metabolism xii, 11
Mold 23, 26, 31
Monosodium Glutamate (MSG) 32
Mortality 4

N

Naturopathics x, xxi, 7, 87, 88, 89, 112
Nervous System 10

O

Obesity 9

P

Parabens 44, 46, 48
Pathogens 71
Pesticides 32
Pills xi, 38, 74, 87, 92

Plastics 6, 24, 28, 39, 45, 50, 53, 55, 56, 57, 109, 110
Pollution
    Air 20, 21, 22, 25
    Automobile Emissions 22
    Carbon Monoxide 22
    Fossil Fuels 21
Polycystic Ovarian Syndrome (PCOS) xvi
Prayer 76, 97
Pregnancy xiii, 74
Preservatives xix, 27, 28, 29, 30, 34, 36
    Types of Common Food Preservatives 30
Probiotics 90
Progesterone 33, 73

R

Recipes 129
Recombinant Bovine Somatotropin (rBST) 33
Reproduction 11

S

Sauna , 107, 107
Secondhand Smoke 24
Sleep , 92, 92
Styrofoam 56, 57
Sulfites 31
Supplements , 69, 87, 88, 72, 90, 90
    Nutritional and Herbal Supplements , 69, 87, 88, 72, 90, 90

T

Teflon 54
Television 93
Testosterone 33
Thyroid 10
Tobacco Use 25
Toxic Exposures
    in the Workplace 22
    Smoke 24, 25
Toxins iii, vii, xvi, xvii, xix, xx, xxi, 3, 5, 6, 7, 8, 9, 11, 20, 21, 22, 23, 25, 28, 25, 37, 33, 50, 40, 51, 38, 42, 48, 49, 52, 54, 69, 61, 55, 57, 66, 69, 70, 70, 82, 72, 73, 74, 75, 87, 88, 90, 91, 93, 94, 107, 108, 95
    In Household Products 51
    In Personal Care Products 44
    Relationships 58, 61
Trans Fats 32

U

Urethra 69
US Environmental Protection Agency (EPA) 37
US Food and Drug Administration, The 29, 34, 43
Uterus 73, 74, 90, 107

V

Vaginal Steam (V-steam) 106

W

Water
  Recommended Daily Consumption 39
  Spring Water 39, 91
  Tap Water 37
Water, Drinking 37
Weight Loss x, xi, xvi
World Health Organization, The 3, 22

Y

Yoni steam 106